Make th
in
English

TEACH YOURSELF BOOKS

Make the Grade in GCSE English

Don Shiach

TEACH YOURSELF BOOKS

Hodder and Stoughton

First published 1987
Third impression 1988

.

ISBN 0 340 40129 X

Printed in Great Britain for
Hodder and Stoughton Educational,
a division of Hodder and Stoughton Ltd,
Mill Road, Dunton Green, Sevenoaks, Kent,
by Richard Clay Ltd, Bungay, Suffolk.
Photoset by Rowland Phototypesetting Ltd,
Bury St Edmunds, Suffolk

CONTENTS

INTRODUCTION

The GCSE English course

In the GCSE English course, English is seen as a unified subject embracing language *and* literature. There is a separate course in English Literature, but this book is only concerned with *English* and not specifically with English Literature. However, the unified approach to English means the syllabus provides opportunities for sustained reading of *literary* works (e.g. short stories, novels, poetry, autobiography and plays) as well as *non-literary* material such as newspaper articles, reports, statistics and advertisements. Candidates might not sit the separate English Literature examination, therefore, but they are still expected to read widely in preparation for the English exam itself. Indeed, regular reading of books and other material of a sufficiently mature level is one of the most effective ways of improving and extending skills with language.

Oral communication

In the GCSE English course you, as a candidate, will be awarded a grade based on your written work produced under different conditions, as course work and in the examination. However, there is another aspect to the grading system: you have to be assessed also in *Oral Communication*. This is a compulsory part of the English course and it has its own grading scale.

If you are to be awarded a grade in English, you must be assessed and awarded a *separate* grade in Oral Communication. In Oral Communication you will be assessed on a five-point scale from 1 to 5, with grade 1 being the highest level of attainment and grade 5 the lowest. If you are ungraded in Oral Communication, your English award will not be recorded on the GCSE certificate, however high a grade you achieve for your written work.

In other words, you have to achieve, at the very least, a grade 5 award in Oral Communication if your grade in English is to be recognised.

Consider these examples:

A candidate achieves a grade C in English but does not take Oral Communication seriously and is ungraded. The result would be that the grade C in English would not be shown on a GCSE certificate.

A candidate performs well in English and is awarded a B. However, he refuses to turn up for his Oral Communication assessment. Result: no grade in English would be awarded.

Therefore, although Oral Communication is assessed separately from English, it is *compulsory* and an important element. You should take the Oral Communication as seriously as the rest of the English syllabus.

On the GCSE certificate, the English grade will be shown by a letter *and* a number. The letter shows the grade awarded in English and the number the grade awarded in Oral Communication. Apart from the fact that you cannot be awarded a grade in English unless you achieve at least a grade 5 in Oral Communication, it is important that you achieve a good result in this part of the examination, to show that you are skilled in communicating in spoken English.

Examinations and course work

Except for external or private candidates who will not be able to submit course work as part of their overall assessment, all candidates must submit course work which must comprise at least 20 per cent of the total assessment. (Some English syllabuses allow you to submit 100 per cent course work.)

Some examining boards offer alternative methods of assessment. You can either sit an examination paper on a particular aspect of English (e.g. Understanding and Response) or submit a coursework folder consisting of a certain number of units of writing showing your understanding and response to various kinds of material.

Which option of assessment you choose – examination or course work – in particular sections of the syllabus will be a matter of discussion between you and your teacher. Remember, however, unless you are a private or external candidate, you have to submit a certain proportion of course work to be assessed. The advice given in the chapters that follow is meant to apply both to preparing for written examinations *and* course work. In addition, we give advice about how to get the best results from your coursework submissions.

English is particularly suitable for continuous assessment through course work. In the opinion of many teachers, examiners and candidates, course work provides a fairer basis for assessing a candidate's abilities than a particular performance in one examination. But remember that course work is not a 'soft' or 'easy' alternative to examinations: consistent, hard work is required to produce course work in English that will earn you the highest possible grade award.

What you are being tested on
In GCSE English you will be tested on your ability to:

> understand and convey information;
> understand, order and present facts, ideas and opinions;
> consider information in reading material of various kinds and select
>   what is relevant for specific purposes;
> express yourself imaginatively in writing and speaking;
> understand meaning and attitudes that are suggested in a written form;
> respond to extracts from literary works or to complete texts;
> show a sense of audience and how to adapt spoken and written English
>   to formal and informal situations;
> show command of grammar, punctuation, spelling, paragraphing and
>   sentence structure in your writing;
> communicate appropriately and effectively in spoken English.

One of the important points that must be stressed is the need to write and speak in an appropriate style or 'voice' for particular purposes and situations – this is what is meant by having a 'sense of audience'. We will return to this point frequently in the chapters that follow.

Types of writing
You will be tested on your ability to write continuously either in an examination paper or by submitting an Expression or Continuous Writing coursework folder. You will be expected to write in a variety of *modes* (i.e. to write in various styles) and forms: narrative, personal, argumentative, descriptive, explanatory.

Within the Expression or Continuous Writing paper or coursework category, a distinction will be made between 'open' and 'closed' (or '*directed*') writing. 'Open' writing is the freer, more personal or imaginative writing; 'closed' writing is more specific, for particular purposes such as writing a letter, a statement, a report or a summary. In the Understanding and Response section of the GCSE course, you will be presented with one or two passages which could be: a newspaper article, an extract from imaginative writing, a complete short story, an extract from an autobiography, factual articles, or contrasting accounts of events.

You might then be asked questions of various types. For example, you may be asked to extract information, summarise relevant sections, read between the lines, analyse meaning and attitudes, or express feelings and opinions.

You might also be asked to write a piece of *directed writing* arising out of the original material – for example, writing a letter for a specific audience and for a particular purpose, or writing a publicity leaflet. We will go into much more detail in the 'Understanding' chapter about the kinds of tasks you will have to cope with, but bear in mind that there is much more to 'understanding' given material than just extracting information and giving it back to the examiner.

As we have seen, your examining board may offer course work as an alternative to an examination paper in Understanding and Response. For assessment by the examiners, the course work will have to consist of a definite number of units of work which will be specified in the syllabus. These units of work should show your ability to understand and respond to extracts from literature *and* whole books, as well as articles and reports.

The writing might show your ability to analyse, explain or give opinions on the extracts or works of literature. The writing could be in the form of an imaginative response to the texts: you could write personally or creatively, as long as the starting-point for the writing is clearly the text that has been studied. Another type of writing that is acceptable is where you write about a number of texts (whole books or a collection of shorter pieces) centred round a common theme or by the same author.

The final units of work submitted in the coursework folder should be carefully chosen to reflect the *best* of your work done during the course.

These pages have given you a brief introduction to the GCSE English course. It will all become much clearer in the chapters that follow, where there is plenty of useful advice and material for practising your language skills. Almost always, tasks are set at the end of each section. Do these as thoroughly as possible. Don't sell yourself short by peeking at the sample answers and neglecting to do your own writing, or by looking up the answers at the back of the book.

It is *your* future. It is *your* exam. By working your way through this book and following the advice given, you could substantially improve your chances of gaining a good grade in GCSE English. It is up to you.

MAKING THE GRADE

It is a well known saying that 'examinations test candidates' ability to sit examinations'. By this it is meant that examinations are not really about examining what you know or the skills you possess, but simply test how well you perform *in the examination room*.

Like most popular sayings, there is a grain of truth amidst the exaggeration in the statement. Success in examinations does *partly* depend on your skills in adapting yourself to examination conditions – but only partly.

'I'm hopeless at examinations' How often do you hear people say that! Perhaps you have said it about yourself. In our opinion, falling back on the excuse that you're hopeless at examinations is a cop-out. It is just a way of excusing yourself in advance for failure. In fact, it's a way of preparing yourself for failure, so banish such thoughts from your mind.

Course work and exams

Course work represents a very important part of your GCSE English course. Some of you may even be assessed wholly on course work and not be required to sit an examination as such, although some of the writing produced for your coursework submission may have to be done in supervised conditions in school or college.

Course work relies on continuous assessment, i.e. your work is being assessed throughout the English course, although the final folder of your best work has to be re-assessed at the end of the course. The best attitude to take is to approach each unit of writing you do for the course work as if it were writing you were doing in an actual exam. After all, course work is like a continuous examination of your skills in English.

But sitting an actual examination, taking a paper in English, does require particular techniques and it is surprising how many candidates fail to do themselves justice by ignoring essential examination rules and techniques.

In the examination room

It may seem very obvious, but we must remind you of the need to arrive outside the exam room several minutes before the official start of the exam. Plan your journey carefully to arrive in good time (but not *too* early).

Make absolutely sure you know the exact days and starting times of all your exams. Have an adult or a friend check the dates and times with you well before the exams start.

Check beforehand that you have all the writing equipment, etc., you need for the exam. If you are permitted a dictionary, use one you are thoroughly familiar with.

Listen to all the instructions from the person in charge of the examination very carefully. Once you are in the exam room, focus your attention entirely on the exam. No talking is allowed once you enter an exam room.

It does not matter what your friends are doing or how they are coping during the exam. For two or three hours be entirely single-minded and selfish in your goals.

The examination paper

Read all the instructions on the examination paper very carefully. If you are given a reading period before the writing of the exam begins, then use that time to the full. Do not just scan the paper briefly and then spend the rest of the reading period staring into space. If you have a choice of questions, check how many you have to answer and decide which ones you will tackle.

Nothing in the examination paper should come as a real surprise to you. Even if there are some questions that seem rather tricky, do not allow yourself to despair. Try and cope as well as you can.

Read the questions very carefully. Look for key words that tell you what the examiners are looking for:

Analyse why . . .
Discuss the reasons for . . .
Imagine you are the person who receives the letter and write . . .
Compare the motives of . . .
Summarise in your own words . . .
From your own experience, write about a time . . .
Between lines 3 and 15, what *evidence* is there for . . .
Give the meaning of . . .
Choose one of the following topics . . .
From paragraph 3 of the extract what do we learn about . . .
List the items that . . .
Consider the opinions expressed by. . . . *Express your opinion* about the issue.
Using examples from the passage, show what is meant by . . .
Either write a letter *or* a straightforward account of . . .

Always pinpoint exactly what the question is asking you to do and answer accordingly: you will not gain extra marks for doing *more* than the question specifies, but you will lose marks if you don't answer it fully.

Look out for questions that are sub-divided into sections or parts – e.g. 6(*a*) . . . (*b*) . . . (*c*) . . . Unless otherwise indicated, you should answer all parts of a question.

Time

In most English papers where there is more than one section, it is usually indicated how long you should spend on particular sections:

'You should spend about an hour on this section.'
'You should spend 30 minutes on this part.'

Always take the advice given by the examiners about time. The time spent on any one section of a paper is linked to the 'mark weighting', i.e. the number of marks which have been allocated to each section.

The same rule applies to individual questions and the mark weightings they receive. This is usually indicated in brackets after each question – e.g. (10), (3), (5) – and indicates how long an answer you are expected to write, or how many separate points you should make (e.g. in arguing a case).

Aim to write at a brisk pace, not in a headlong rush, and always leave a few minutes at the end of each section of a paper to check over what you have written. It is surprising what errors, and how many, you can make in the heat of examination writing. Spend time checking your work, and correcting any careless errors, and you will not lose marks unnecessarily.

Handwriting

Examiners are human. They prefer legible and neat handwriting. Although they will swear that difficult handwriting does not influence their assessment of an exam paper, research has shown that teachers in general reward more favourably those pupils whose handwriting is neat and attractive.

If you have a problem with your handwriting, then do something about it well before you have to sit the exams. You cannot suddenly change it overnight. It has to be a gradual and conscious change to complete legibility. This is also important in the presentation of your course work.

A whole chapter is devoted to accuracy – of spelling, grammar, punctuation and sentence construction – because it is very important in the writing sections of the GCSE English course. You cannot afford to lose marks by making careless errors which, with effort and practice, you *can* avoid.

In general, however interesting a piece of writing is and however well-structured and expressed it may be, it will not receive a good mark if the spelling is poor. Spelling accuracy is an important factor in the success, or otherwise, of all candidates taking GCSE English. Examiners *do* pay considerable attention to spelling accuracy, so you must pay attention to it too. The world outside school and college also expects you to be able to spell accurately.

Too many people shake their heads, wring their hands and say, 'I just can't spell!'. However, it is a fact that you *can* do something positive to improve your spelling, but it does take determined effort on your part. Examiners usually divide spelling errors into two main categories: firstly, errors in the spelling of very common words and secondly, mistakes in spelling more difficult words. The minimum aim you should set yourself is to avoid the misspelling of the most common words.

You can improve your spelling by reading as much as possible. Reading words over and over in books, magazines and newspapers will help you recognise the patterns of letters in words.

However, there is no real substitute for using words themselves in your writing. In addition, saying words aloud and breaking them down into their syllables will help you a great deal.

When you come across a new or unfamiliar word, or a word that you know you have difficulty in spelling, break it down into its separate syllables:

professional	pro/fess/ion/al
necessary	nec/ess/ar/y
legitimate	le/git/i/mate

Of course, whenever possible, you should refer to a dictionary to check the spelling of words of which you are unsure. Make out your own lists of difficult words in alphabetical order in a notebook. Whenever you receive a piece of work back from a teacher, note the spelling errors that have been marked and do your corrections.

Some examining boards allow you to take dictionaries into an exam; this is very useful, but you cannot spend all your time looking up words.

Simple errors
As we have already said there are some very simple, but fairly common, spelling errors that examiners frown on, because candidates at GCSE should know how to spell all of these words. These are some of them:

their   there   they're
Their parents were waiting for them at the gates.
There is nothing we can do about it.
They're (they are) not the kind of people we like.

know   no
I don't know what you're talking about.
Yes, we have no bananas.

were   where   we're
We were at a loss to know what to do next.
Where are we going to find somewhere to live?
We're (=we are) not going to give in.

its   it's
The dog licked its mouth.
It's (=it is) no use crying over spilt milk.

past   passed
He walked past the shop three times.
He passed the shop three times.
In the past, kings and queens were much more powerful.

whole   hole
Do you swear to tell the whole truth and nothing but the truth?
The rabbit disappeared down the hole.

You may think these words are far too easy for you to misspell them, but examiners know only too well that many candidates do.

Exercise   In the following sentences there are numerous incorrect uses of simple words mentioned above. Rewrite the passage correcting the errors. (For answers see p. 172.)

1 'It's time to get up,' ~~there~~ *their* mother shouted from downstairs.
2 'Their's no need to shout. We're not late,' said Jack.
3 'The cat is wagging its tail,' said Bill. 'That shows its annoyed.'
4 'I don't ~~no~~ *know* – you're mad! ~~Were~~ *Where* are my shoes? They ~~where~~ *were* under my
    bed. It's a real mystery to me ~~they~~ *where* they get to every morning. I spend a
    ~~hole~~ *whole* hour looking for them. Look at the time – it's half ~~passed~~ *past* eight. It's
    well past the time when I ~~should have~~ *should've* left for school.'

Words often confused
There are several more common words that are frequently confused with one another despite their simplicity. When an examiner spots these errors, it makes a bad impression, so use these words with special care.

to   too   two
I went to the cinema. (*preposition: to*)
It was too hot for my liking. (*adverb: too*)
I bought two cakes. (*number: two*)

here   hear

Here are the newspapers you wanted.

It's very restful living down here.

I hear you're moving house.

Can you hear me?

who   who's   whose

Who is coming to lunch? (or) Who's coming to lunch?

The person who is sitting on your right hand side is your partner for this game.

He's the man who's causing all the trouble.

Whose house is this anyway? (To whom does this house belong?)

I know whose book this is. (belonging to)

Below are some examples of slightly less common words that are often confused. These words sound the same but are spelt differently and have different meanings.

accept   except

I accept this great honour you are bestowing on me.

Except for me, there is no one left.

I have no excuse except that the bus was late.

affect   effect

Drugs affect your health badly.

Does this affect how you feel about me?

The effect of drugs on your health is serious.

I would like to effect some changes.

board   bored

What we need is a flat board of some kind.

The film bored me stiff.

bough   bow

He was swinging on the bough of a tree.

I'll bow my head to no man.

He strung the arrow in the bow.

cereal   serial

I like only one cereal for breakfast and that's muesli.

I enjoy an exciting serial on the radio.

conscious   conscience

I am very conscious that I am in your debt.

Is the boxer conscious yet after that terrible knockout?

I am not guilty, so my conscience is clear.

current   currant

How many currants have you put into this pudding?

Go out and get the current edition of *Who's Who*.

He was swept away by the river's current.

Exercise In each of the following sentences there is at least one word incorrectly used. Write out the corrected version of each of the sentences. (For answers see p. 172.)

1 I no who's tie that is. *KNOW*
2 He's to tired two talk too more than too people at a time. *TOO TO TWO*
3 I can here you very well, although the line isn't to good. Whose is it whose talking? *HEAR TOO*
4 You can except or not except, that's entirely up to you, accept that there is a certain amount of urgency two settle this matter, as you no. *ACCEPT ACCEPT EXCEPT THERE'S TO KNOW*
5 The affect of your doing that would be to effect what I'm doing. *EFFECT AFFECT*
6 He seemed board all evening and nearly fell asleep over the games bored. *BORED BOARDS*
7 To bough to someone is not a sign of weakness. *BOW*
8 The last episode of the cereal was recorded by them on their video and they watched it next morning at breakfast while eating their serial. *SERIAL CEREAL*
9 What he did must be on his conscious. *CONSCIENCE*
10 I am very conscience that I have made a mistake. *CONSCIOUS*
11 The currant situation is that there is no news at the moment. *CURRENT THERE'S*
12 Put some more currents in this cake. *CURRANTS*

In the following passage there are numerous spelling errors of common words. Write out the passage again with these errors corrected. (For answers see p. 172.)

He was not conscience when they brought him too the hospital. That much I new. I was standing their when I happened to here to doctors talking about his currant state of health. *CONSCIOUS TO KNEW THERE HEAR TWO CURRENT*

'Whose going two operate?' I could here one doctor say. *TO HEAR*

'There's know one on duty accept for Johnstone; I must say, if I where him, I wouldn't be too confident.' *NO EXCEPT WERE*

After hering that, I stood with boughed head. The fact that he was lying in hospital close too death lay heavily on my conscious. Who's fault was it? I couldn't except that I was entirely free of blame. If only he hadn't board me so much, but that was how he managed to effect me. The question now was what affect the operation would have on him. I knew that it would effect me. *HEARING BOWED TO CONSCIENCE WHOSE ACCEPT BORED AFFECT EFFECT AFFECT*

More tricky words
Here are more words that are commonly confused:

desert dessert
The desert stretched before them over miles and miles of sand.
He got his just deserts.
For dessert there was apple pie.

5 Spelling

lay   lie
We have come to lay the carpet.
She asked us to lie hidden in the corner.
Don't lie to me.

loose   lose
The knot in the string was very loose.
They knew they were going to lose the game.

peace   piece
We hope for peace, not war.
I would like a piece of that cake.

practice   practise
The practice takes place every evening at seven. (practice: noun)
Remember to practise every day (practise: verb)

receipt   recipe
If you do not have your receipt, then I cannot give you the money back.
It was a very complicated Italian recipe which I could not follow.

weather   whether
The weather is going to be lovely today.
I asked him whether there was any hope of survival.

through   thorough   threw (or throw)
To get to Maxton, you have to pass through Selford.
His preparation was very thorough.
I threw the ball at him.
Can I throw this at the window?

Exercise The following passage has frequent examples of the words dealt
with in this section being wrongly used. Rewrite the passage inserting the
correct words for the context. (For answers see p. 172.)

A receipt for piece is hard to find. No country wants to lose territory,
weather or not its claim is just. Only threw patient negotiation and
practise can we hope to achieve any breakthrough. Weather or not we
can do so, we cannot but be very through in our efforts to put into
practise what we preach. We preach piece but prepare to make the
world a dessert threw nuclear war. We must not lie down impossible
conditions for our so-called enemies and expect them to lay down
while we trample all over their rights. Until each nation is in recipe of
binding rules for pieceful co-existence, then there is no hope for the
world and we will all get our just desserts.

Useful words

Here is an alphabetical list of useful words which are commonly misspelt.

accidentally accommodation across address advertisement already among
ancestor animal annoyed appearance attitude authority awkward
beautiful because bicycle biscuit building business
calendar capable career caution challenge character cigarette coffee
conscientious continually cupboard
definite delicious disappointing discouraged
electricity embarrassment exaggerate exception excitement exhilarate
experience experiment explanation extraordinary extremely
families family favourite February financial foreign foreigners furniture
generous gorgeous government gradually guardian guile guilt guise guitar
honesty honour humorous humour hurriedly
immediately impossible impudence incredible independence independent
ingenious initial innocent intrigue invention invincible invisible island
jewellery junior
language lawyer league leaves leisure library lieutenant logical loneliness
magical majority mantelpiece manufacture marriage material mayor
mechanically menial millionaire miracle miscellaneous mission musical
mysterious
natural naturally necessary neighbourhood noticeable numerous
obstacle obviously occurred offend operation opportunity oxygen
paragraph parallel passion patience payment pension periodically phase
philosophy photograph physical picturesque poise popular possessions
practical precious precipitate prefer preference preferred pregnant prejudice
preparation prepare preposterous process procession procure produce
production professional programme prohibit projector prolong pronounce
propaganda property proportion protection puncture pyjamas
quantity query quota
radiator rally ration rebel receipt reception recipe recommend regional
relevant relieved religious restaurant rhyme rhythm ridiculous route ruin
Saturday scarcely scent schedule scheme science scientific scintillating
scissors selection signal signalled similar simultaneous spectacles stomach
stories storeys succeed successful sufficient suggestion summer
superstitious surprising suspicious sympathy
taste temperature tempting terrifying terror threaten threshold thrilling
thwarted tobacco tolerance touching tractor train tranquil transistor travelled
tremendous triumph truant truly typical
unbecoming unbelievable uncontrolled unconventional undeniable
underrated understanding unnecessary unnerving upsetting
vacancy vacuum vague vain valid valuable vandal vandalize vanity variable
variation variety various vary vegetable vehement vein veneer vengeance
venue verdict verify vertical vestige veterinary veto viable vicarious vicious
victim victimize victory video view viewpoint vigour village villain vindicated
violent virtue visual vitality vivacious vivid vociferous voluntary volunteer
vow voyage vulnerable
wanton warranty wastage wasteful weapon welfare whenever whereas wilful
withdrawn witticism woollen worthless wrath wreathed wreckage wretched
writhe   yearn yield   zeal zest

Accurate punctuation is just as important as accurate spelling. Punctuation is a necessity; it is not an optional extra. Without adequate punctuation a piece of writing can become jumbled and very difficult to understand. Undoubtedly examiners will judge your ability to punctuate your writing, so you must pay attention to it.

Sentences and end-stopping
Sentences begin with a capital letter and end with a full stop, just as this sentence has.

Examiners know only too well that numerous candidates seem unable to recognise where one sentence ends and another begins. These candidates too often allow sentences to run into one another, so that there are few of the definite breaks or stops that the flow of meaning clearly requires.

The placing of full stops is vital to a reader's understanding of any piece of continuous writing. Some people refer to this as 'end-stopping', which means deciding where a definite stop (i.e. the end of a sentence) should be made. If a candidate shows little or no awareness of *end-stopping*, then an examiner is bound to mark him or her down.

Commas instead of full stops
A major fault is to have a succession of weak commas when you should be using strong full stops. Read this short passage aloud:

> The audience at the rock concert were very excited, there was almost pandemonium when the star came on stage; he was dressed in a bright red suit with spangles, some people thought he looked quite vulgar, the most enthusiastic of his fans, however, thought he looked great, most of the audience stood and cheered.

When you read that aloud, you should have noticed definite breaks in the flow of meaning when one statement has been made and another begins. It is at those points where commas are not sufficient; definite breaks in the flow of meaning need to be signposted for the reader by end-stopping, i.e. by the use of a full stop. Thus, in the above passage, most of the commas should have been replaced by full stops to mark where one sentence ends and another begins.

More about end-stopping
When you have written a piece of continuous writing, read it over to yourself, mentally listening to the sense and checking that every one of your sentences begins with a capital letter and ends with a full stop. Guard against the sin of 'comma-itis', i.e. using a succession of weak commas instead of strong full stops.

Exercise Read through the following passages (saying them aloud to yourself). Decide where full stops should be inserted – where, for example, an item of punctuation is missing or where a comma has been used incorrectly in place of a full stop, then rewrite the passages. (For answers see p. 173.)

1 When winter comes, birds fall on hard times some kind people leave food out for these hardy types that remain behind however, many small birds die during the harsh wintry months if more people were thoughtful enough, more of those lovely small creatures would survive.

2 At that time there was a great deal of industrial trouble some people were calling for a general strike others wanted settlement by negotiation the result was chaos millions of people were involved those not on strike were affected anyway the atmosphere in the country was very unsettled.

3 Of all the films released that Christmas, there was no doubt as to which was the most popular, science fiction films were big box-office at that time and this particular example of the genre really drew the crowds, some of the critics did not review the film very favourably the public, however, voted with their money, the makers of the film became millionaires almost overnight.

4 Jane couldn't keep up with all the latest dance crazes one would appear from America, followed by yet another, no sooner had she learned to do one dance than she felt she had to learn a new dance, Jane prided herself in being up-to-date, she hated the idea of not knowing what the latest thing was.

5 The rain poured down the umpires had no hesitation in stopping play, the crowd, however, thought differently they booed the decision, after all, they had paid good money for their match tickets a little rain was no obstacle to play in their eyes.

Semi-colons

The semi-colon (;) can be used as an alternative to the full stop. It marks a stop in the flow of the sense, more definite than a comma, but not so definite as a full stop. The semi-colon's main function is to break a long sentence into sections, as in this example:

> The flat was quite spacious; it had four rooms, a kitchen and a bathroom.

Obviously, the two parts of this sentence are closely connected. There could be a full stop after 'spacious' and a new sentence could begin there, but the semi-colon is a useful alternative. A comma separating the two parts would definitely be wrong.

Please note that what follows a semi-colon should form a proper, complete statement, i.e. not a phrase, nor an incomplete sentence:

It was a wonderful Christmas; everyone had a marvellous time.

The musicians played like demons; it was obvious that the famous conductor had inspired them.

The street was narrow and dark; along one side stood some dingy, terraced houses; opposite were some factory-type buildings.

A candidate who can use semi-colons properly and appropriately will impress the examiners.

Colons

A colon (:) can be used when the first part of a sentence leads into a list:

Arthur Miller wrote several important plays: *Death of a Salesman*, *A View from a Bridge*, *The Crucible* and *All My Sons*.

It is also used when the second part of a sentence defines, amplifies or explains the first part:

There are two main reasons for the Government's unpopularity: high inflation and unemployment.

A colon can also introduce a quotation:

Oscar Wilde coined many famous epigrams such as: 'Work is the curse of the drinking classes'.

Exercise In the following passages there are opportunities for using semi-colons and/or colons. Sometimes commas are used incorrectly and should be replaced by semi-colons or colons. Rewrite each passage inserting semi-colons or colons where appropriate. (For answers see p. 173.)

1 The play consisted of three sections; these were a prologue, a main act and an epilogue.
2 The production also required a large cast, two leading actors, twelve supporting roles and three children.
3 The Minister explained his decision; there was no money available; the government was against it anyway; there seemed to be no demand for it.
4 The politician was quoted as saying; 'I have no intention of resigning.'
5 The teacher told the pupils what they had to supply; walking boots, anoraks, tents, sleeping bags and basic utensils. There were to be no exceptions; everybody had to supply his own.

Punctuating direct speech

Direct speech is a speaker's actual words:

'I'm not at all sorry,' she said.

The actual words spoken are enclosed within speech marks or inverted commas. You can use single (' ') or double (" ") inverted commas.

Usually the actual words someone speaks are followed by a comma before the speech marks are closed if something like 'he said' or 'she replied' is used.

'We're going to the pictures,' she replied.

Generally you will be using direct speech in narrative or personal writing. When you write a stretch of direct speech, you should remember to start a new paragraph each time there is a change of speaker:

'Look, this is our last chance,' she protested.
'I can't do anything about that. It's out of my hands,' he apologised.
'Can't you do anything?' she insisted.
'I wish I could.'

Another important point to note is the punctuation you should use when 'he said', etc., comes in the middle of the direct speech.

(*a*) 'I feel ill,' he said, 'so I'm going home now.'
(*b*) 'That's not my fault,' she said. 'Blame someone else for a change.'

In (*a*) there is a comma after 'ill'; another comma, rather than a full stop, appears after 'said' because the speaker is completing what he has to say in the same sentence. Note that the speech marks are closed after 'ill', and then reopened following the comma after 'he said'.

In (*b*) the second part of what she says is a separate sentence, so it starts with a capital letter and there is a full stop after 'said'.

Exercises The following passages contain direct speech, but essential punctuation has been missed out. Rewrite the passages inserting the correct punctuation. (For answers see p. 173.)

1 Why? Joan demanded. Why does it always have to be me? Because it's the woman's role Jack said Is it now? Joan exploded In which book of rules did you read that? It's the way of things Jack replied Well, I'm not your mother nor your sister Joan stated so cook your own dinner.

2 What is your secret as a striker, Bert? the commentator asked Is it your eye for a half-chance? I've always been quick, Bert said I think on my feet, if you know what I mean. Sharp as mustard. You are that, the commentator agreed. Do you ever feel down after a game? Sick as a parrot, David, sick as a parrot. But then he continued I feel over the moon at other times.

3 I feel depressed Bill said Depressed, depressed, depressed. We all get depressed Alec said What's so different about you? I have more reason to be depressed Bill continued because I'm broke. I haven't a job and I have to share this flat with you. Charming! Alec protested. Well, you know what you can do. I might just do that said Bill.

Grammar is a way of describing a language. Grammatical terms are used about particular kinds of words (e.g. *nouns*, *verbs*, *adjectives*, *adverbs*) or about the *relationship* between words (e.g. *subject* of the *verb*, *object* of the *verb*, *relative clause*).

Grammar tends to be thought of as a set of rules that must be applied to the language; in fact, different dialects of the same language can have different sets of grammatical rules which are unique to those dialects and, therefore, correct as far as those dialects are concerned. However, the fact is that GCSE English generally tests your ability to write Standard English, not dialects of English, or colloquial English. Therefore you must be able to write according to the grammatical conventions applying to Standard English – the kind of English you read in books, hear on the radio and television and see in newspapers and magazines and in official communications. If you repeatedly make mistakes of a grammatical kind in your writing of Standard English, you will lose marks in an examination or course work.

You must be able to write consistently in complete, properly constructed sentences. You must also be able to write in longer, more complex sentences as well as in simple sentences consisting of one statement. If your sentence construction is unvaried, monotonous and limited in its complexity, you will not impress the examiner. Try to vary the *types* and *lengths* of sentences.

Simple sentences
Simple sentences make one statement and have one verb:

The rain *fell* from the dark clouds.

The italicised word is the verb – the word in the sentence that describes the action. Verbs are not always words of action. There is the very common verb *to be* with all its different parts:

am   is   are   was   were   be   been   is being

Then there are such verbs as *look*, *seem*, *appear*, *become*, *feel*, *have*, which do not imply an action.

Subject-verb agreement
Every sentence needs one verb at least and the verb has *to agree with* the subject of the sentence:

The shoppers were crowding round the counter.

'Shoppers', the subject of the sentence and those carrying out the action ('were crowding'), is plural and therefore needs a plural form of the verb: 'were'.

A common error is the failure to make the subject and verb agree:

The shoppers was crowding round the counter.   ×

Plural subjects require plural verbs; singular subjects have singular verbs.

The loudspeakers was far too loud.   ×
The loudspeakers were far too loud.   √

No one have left the room.   ×
No one has left the room.   √

Thousands of people is standing out in the cold.   ×
Thousands of people are standing out in the cold.   √

Collective nouns

A **collective noun** is the name for a group of people or things:

crowd   committee   team   government   council

There are also collective nouns used to describe groups of animals:
herd   pride (of lions)   flock

Collective nouns may be followed by either a singular or a plural verb:

(*a*)   The crowd *is* very important at any big game.
(*b*)   The crowd *are* very angry at that decision.

(*a*)   The committee *meets* every Wednesday.
(*b*)   The committee *were amazed* by the information.

In both (*a*) sentences the collective nouns – crowd and committee – refer to the group as a whole and therefore take a singular verb.

In both (*b*) sentences 'crowd' and 'committee' mean all the individual members (i.e. more than one member) and therefore take a plural verb.

Exercise   Read the following passages aloud. Some 'sentences' in the passages are not really sentences at all, because the verbs have been incorrectly left out. Other sentences have incorrect subject-verb agreement. Rewrite the passages inserting suitable verbs and correcting the grammatical errors. (For answers see p. 174.)

1   Juvenile delinquency are on the increase, we is reliably informed. What, then, are the single main cause for this increase? Perhaps parents no longer control their children. Perhaps children themselves has changed. Or have the period we are living through changed so rapidly that young people confused by the pace of it all? Whatever the reasons, it seems that the authorities is genuinely concerned. Juvenile delinquents, however, is not a new phenomenon. There has always been complaints about the sins of the younger generation, who in turn become the next generation to complain about the young. It appear it will always be the same.

2 Moving day were an ordeal for the family. First of all, the van were late. The glass on some picture frames were broken and the cats was reluctant to leave their home. The van men not particularly co-operative. It appear they was not really interested in helping. Their time costed enough, that were for sure. Eventually, it were all sorted out and the family to move house.

3 Cats is funny animals. They have tremendous pride and shows an independence few human beings has. Some people looks down on cats. Because their brains is said to be small. However, the fact is that they possesses a native intelligence, a cunning, an alertness, that alone make them in some ways even more intelligent than humans.

Joining sentences

We have already stated that it is necessary to write in a variety of types and lengths of sentences. To illustrate the point, read this succession of short, simple sentences:

> I am writing this book. I want to write a section on joining sentences. I am doing that now. I am writing in a very boring style. I am repeating the same kind of sentence structure. I am boring myself by doing this.

There are six simple sentences in that paragraph. A simple sentence is a sentence that makes one statement and has one verb:

> I am writing this book.

Notice too that the same construction is repeated six times:

> I am writing . . .   I want to . . .   I am doing . . .
> I am writing . . .   I am repeating . . .   I am boring . . .

Repetition of similar constructions becomes extremely monotonous; the lack of variety in the length of sentences is also tedious. Read this short passage:

> The rain poured all day. Play was out of the question. The umpires called it off. They had no real choice.

These four simple sentences can be made into one by using joining words in this way:

> As the rain had poured all day and play was out of the question, the umpires called it off because they had no real choice.

Joining words such as those used here – 'and', 'as', 'because' – are called **conjunctions**. The most common conjunctions are:

> although and as after before because but if nor or
> since so that though that till until unless

Conjunctions are used to combine simple sentences into a **complex sentence** or a **compound sentence**.

A complex sentence is a sentence with one **main** or **principal clause** (the clause that makes the main statement of the sentence) and one or more **subordinate** or **dependent** clauses. The main clause of a sentence is the *part that could stand on its own* and make sense without any additions. In the above sentence the main clause is 'the umpires called it off'. There are three other clauses in the sentence which are subordinate to, or dependent on, this main clause, and each is joined to the rest of the sentence by a conjunction.

'But', 'and' and 'or' are used to join simple sentences together into compound sentences. Compound sentences are sentences that consist of *two or more main clauses*; in other words, both, or all of, the clauses of a compound sentence could stand on their own and make sense without any additions. Below are some illustrations of how to use 'but', 'and' and 'or':

He wanted to do it. He couldn't.
He wanted to do it, *but* he couldn't.
There were only four classrooms available. Two hundred pupils had enrolled for the term.
There were only four classrooms available *and* two hundred pupils had enrolled for the term.
They could have responded. They could have done nothing.
They could have responded *or* done nothing.

A sign of mature writing skill is the ability to write in longer, complex sentences when the need arises. Of course, there are times when a succession of short sentences is appropriate to the purpose or tone of a piece of writing. For example, a series of short, crisp sentences can be very effective in building up tension in describing an action sequence:

She hesitated. What could she do? The shadow moved again in the room. Carefully she pulled out the gun. She cocked the trigger. Her eyes were growing accustomed to the dark. She could see the figure more clearly. It was Mark Grayson!

Generally, however, you will want to write in a variety of sentence lengths. Conjunctions are essential tools in writing these complex sentences.

Exercise Below are groups of simple sentences. Use conjunctions to join each group into one complex sentence, or, at the most, two. (For answers see p. 174.)

1 The animals were restless. They knew their feeding time to the very minute. They seemed to have an in-built instinct about it.
2 There was no obvious reason for his anger. The pupils were surprised by it. They felt guilty. They had done nothing.

3 The passengers waited patiently for the bus. The bus was very late. The snow and ice had made the roads treacherous. Cars were sliding all over the place. Driving was an extremely hazardous business.
4 The soap opera was extremely popular with the public. It had plenty of dramatic climaxes and colourful characters. It brought some weekly excitement into very drab lives. The programme reached the top of the viewing figures. People of all ages watched it. It was written to have a wide appeal.
5 Fashion is a business. That's why fashions have to change frequently. Designers and clothes manufacturers profit from this. It is obvious.

Relative pronouns

Another important and useful part of speech in joining up sentences is the **relative pronoun**. The relative pronouns are:

who whom whose	Use *who*, *whom* and *whose* when referring to people.
which	Use *which* when referring to things.
that	Use *that* (never *what*) when referring to things and, sometimes, people.

Here are some illustrations of how and where relative pronouns are used:

There was a house for sale. I wanted desperately to buy it.
There was a house for sale *which* I wanted desperately to buy.

He was a kind man. He would do anything for anyone.
He was a kind man *who* would do anything for anyone.

She was a very cheerful type of person. Everyone liked her.
She was a very cheerful type of person *whom* everyone liked.

These are the pupils. Their books have been lost.
These are the pupils *whose* books have been lost.

The gold jewellery was very valuable. There was no trace of it.
The gold jewellery, *of which* there was no trace, was very valuable.

There is the building. I bought it.
There is the building *that* I bought.

These relative pronouns are used to introduce **adjectival clauses**. They are called adjectival clauses because they describe something about a noun or a pronoun in the previous clause.

You can quite often omit a relative pronoun when it is the object of the adjectival clause:

This sounds like something (that) we will enjoy.
He was a man (whom) everyone respected.

The important thing is to be able to construct complex sentences using relative pronouns: you can then omit them if you like *when it is grammatically correct to do so.*

Exercise Below are groups of sentences. Each group can be joined into one complex sentence by the use of conjunctions and relative pronouns. Rewrite each group as one complex sentence. (For answers see p. 175.)

1 There was no reason. I could not think of one.
2 Quickly she lit the fire. It soon heated up the room.
3 He spoke about France. He knew nothing about it. This infuriated her. She knew much more.
4 United had to win the final game. It was against the City. They were fourth in the league. They had been playing very badly. This had surprised no one.
5 The woman was wearing a red coat. She disappeared quickly from the store. It was in Oxford Street. It was very busy at that time.
6 The lawyer arranged the purchase of the house. He was very efficient. The house was in Broomhill Road. It was in a very quiet district.

Common grammatical errors
Compound subjects
In the sentence

He and I were both present that morning.

the subject of the sentence – 'he and I' – is an example of a *compound subject*. When the subject of a sentence consists of two or more singular nouns or pronouns, you must use a plural verb:

The money and the fame were the attractions.

'Money' and 'fame' are joined by 'and' to form the compound subject. The sentence

The money and the fame was the attractions.

would be grammatically wrong.
The examples below show the correct use of compound subjects:

Are he and his friend coming tonight?
The policeman and the criminal were both injured.

Personal pronouns
The personal pronouns are:

I me you he she him her we us they them

The following example illustrates a common error:

He said that you and me ought to go in for the exam.

In this sentence 'you and me' should be replaced by 'you and I' because these pronouns form the compound subject of the clause:

He said that you and I ought to go in for the exam.

Another common error is of this kind:

Me and my friends went to the pictures.

Never use a construction like this in any formal context. You can only really use it in direct speech if it is the manner of speech of a character in a story. The correct version is:

My friends and I went to the pictures.

Here are more illustrations of correct, and incorrect, use of personal pronouns:

That's strictly between you and me. (*Not*: That's strictly between you and I.)
The revolution forced me and James to leave. (*Not*: The revolution forced James and I to leave.)

Misrelated participles
The **present participle** of a verb is the '-ing' form:

running   shouting   greeting   leaving

When using a participle to introduce a phrase, you must be careful to relate the participle to an appropriate subject. If you have a misrelated participle, it can cause all kinds of misunderstanding, for example:

Having only three legs and no drawers, I did not want the table.

This construction makes it appear that the 'I' of the sentence has the 'three legs' and 'no drawers'.
Here is another example:

Having snowed all day, he felt relieved when it stopped.

This sentence makes it seem that 'he' had snowed all day.
Both these sentences would have to be re-structured:

Having only three legs and no drawers, the table was not what I wanted.
He felt relieved when, having snowed all day, it stopped.

Misuse of pronouns
A fairly common error is to mis-match pronouns:

The kids were very angry with himself.   ×
They had hurt himself badly.   ×
We were hugging herself with delight.   ×

The correct versions are:

The kids were very angry with themselves.
They had hurt themselves badly.
We were hugging ourselves with delight.

Exercise   In the following passages there are several errors of the kind we have illustrated here. Rewrite the passages correcting the errors. (For answers see p. 175.)

1   The other boy and me was both very tired. My manager got between I and my opponent; the referee and judge was quick to come to a decision.
2   Between you and they, there are very little to choose. Your education and your natural intelligence gives you an advantage, but they have a street-wise attitude to life. Having had no privileges, the street has taught them to survive. You and me, in comparison, has led very sheltered lives.
3   Having such a rich plumage and a beautiful crested head, the old lady admired the bird. The shopkeeper and the old lady was at loggerheads over the price.

Paragraphing

In your own continuous writing you must use paragraphs correctly and appropriately. Examiners expect you to divide your continuous writing up into paragraphs. These paragraphs separate the content logically into sections; each paragraph deals with one point or aspect of your subject.

In a piece of continuous writing, you ought to deal with one aspect of the subject then move on to another. When you do this, you start a new paragraph.

In direct speech a new paragraph is started each time a different speaker says something. In descriptive, narrative and other forms of continuous writing, however, examiners will be looking for well-developed paragraphs, so think in terms of writing at least three to four sentences per paragraph.

Indenting

In your handwritten work you must *indent*: new paragraphs must be clearly indicated by starting each of them about half an inch from the margin of the paper.

Exercise   The following passages lack paragraphing. Read each passage through and decide where new paragraphs should be started. Consider carefully where there is direct speech involved. The number of paragraphs there should be in each passage is indicated by the number in brackets. (For answers see p. 175.)

1   (5) I am against all blood sports for the obvious reason they are cruel to animals. Human beings seem to think they can practise all kinds of cruelty on animals. This is not so and a growing number of people are actively opposing these sadists. Hunting is one particular hatred of mine. The argument that people need to dress up in red coats and charge across farmland in order to control the spread of foxes is entirely false. These fox-hunters are not performing any social function at all. They are satisfying their own blood-lust. Of course, experiments on animals are among the worst features of cruelty to animals. What goes on in pharmaceutical laboratories defies description. There can be no possible justification for these practices. They should be illegal.

2   (7) 'Let's go the party,' said Maggie despairingly. 'Not another party,' moaned Gerry. It was a familiar argument. Maggie was much more sociable than Gerry, who preferred small gatherings of people. Parties with their blaring music and half-drunk, jostling crowds were his idea of hell. 'You go by yourself. I don't mind,' he said. 'You know I won't go on my own,' Maggie replied. 'That's why you say that. Come on, be a sport – just this once, then I won't ask you again.' 'That's what you always say,' said Gerry. That night they went to the party. Gerry moped in a corner and Maggie did not enjoy herself as much as she had hoped. Neither of them was very pleased with the other.

Continuity

We have already stressed the need to give continuity to your writing. One method of providing this continuity from one paragraph to the next is by the use of *linking words and phrases* (for examples see page 38).

The **demonstrative adjectives** and pronouns 'this' and 'that' can often be used at the beginning of paragraphs to refer back to something that has been stated in the previous paragraph:

> *This* argument can be counteracted by the mention of . . .
> *That*, however, was not of much consolation to Joan.
> *This* surprising turn of events took everyone by surprise.

The general point is that you must consciously provide this kind of continuity for your reader, however you choose to do it. Each new paragraph is, in effect, a signpost which helps the reader to follow the development of your argument or ideas.

Exercise Imagine you are a reporter for a national or local newspaper. Write a report of several paragraphs on one of these:

1 A public meeting (political, an enquiry, community)
2 A ceremonial occasion
3 A performance of a play or a concert of any kind

Pay particular attention to the continuity and how you link the paragraphs.

Tenses
Most narratives use the past tense:

> He opened the door. What a sight met his eyes! He stumbled back in astonishment.

But narratives are sometimes in the present tense:

> He opens the door. What a sight meets his eyes! He stumbles back in astonishment.

However, most candidates find it much more difficult to sustain a narrative in the present tense. Candidates often forget that they have started off in the present tense and change into the past tense for no good reason:

> He tries to speak. He finds words hard to come by. He heard himself say something. She did not reply.

Here the change from the present to the past tense is a major error. Decide the tense in which you are going to tell your story and keep to it. As a general rule, it is safest to choose the past tense for narrative writing.

Reported speech
Some candidates confuse direct speech with reported speech. Direct speech quotes (with speech marks) the actual words of the speaker; reported speech reports the words someone has said, but in narrative form.

In reported speech you must not use speech marks, because you are not quoting the actual words a speaker has used. Because you are reporting them, they will be reported in the past tense.

Exercise Below are some passages that include some direct speech. Rewrite each passage changing the direct speech into reported speech. Consider the tense in which you write the reported speech; do not use speech marks in reported speech. (For answers see p. 175.)

1 'After all, tomorrow is another day,' said Louella.
  'Frankly, my dear, I don't much care for your philosophy,' I replied.
  'Tomorrow will creep in at its own petty pace.'
   'We all have to think of tomorrow,' Louella persisted.
   'I live for the present,' I said.

2 'I could have been a champion,' Rocky said. 'I could have been a contender.'

'You saw some money,' his brother insisted.

'Some money! You don't understand. I could have been somebody. I could've had some class. You should've looked after me Charlie.'

3 'Forward to the past?' Nicky exclaimed. 'You're off your rocker!'

'I know what I'm talking about,' the old man said. 'I have the machine that can fast forward into the past.'

'Rewind to the past, you mean,' Nicky corrected him.

Continuous writing plays an important part in all the GCSE English syllabuses from the various examining boards. As a candidate you may be required to produce for assessment as course work a certain number of writing units as evidence of your ability to write continuously in prose in various 'modes'. Or you may have to sit an examination paper in writing; there are various titles for this type of paper: 'Expression'; 'Continuous Writing'; 'Written Paper'. In addition there are Directed Writing examination papers. Directed Writing, which may also be required for course work, is different from Expression or Continuous Writing in that it is centred round a specific task and for a particular audience (e.g. a letter of complaint to a manufacturer about some appliance you have bought) and arising out of material that is presented to you (e.g. an advertisement, a newspaper article). In Expression or Continuous Writing candidates are usually simply presented with a number of topics and asked to write on one of them.

In this chapter we are concentrating on Expression or Continuous Writing both for course work and examinations. We will deal with Directed Writing in the next chapter.

Assessment
You will be tested on your ability to write in various 'modes', i.e. a variety of types of expressive writing:

narrative (telling a story or giving an account)
personal (writing based on personal experience)
descriptive (describing something, a place or person)
argumentative or **persuasive** (expressing personal opinions)

If you have to submit a coursework folder of expressive writing for assessment, almost certainly you will have to include at least one example from two or three of these modes. In the Expression or Sustained/Continuous Writing exam paper the range of topics will include at least one opportunity to write in each of these modes. You will be assessed on the following aspects of your writing:

the quality of the content;
the organisation of the material;
the use of an appropriate style, tone and language;
the accuracy of the writing;
the command of sentence structure;
the range of expression and vocabulary.

Content

Your writing should show some imagination or arouse the interest of your reader. Examiners and teachers have to read many essays; try to make your writing as interesting as possible to ease their burdens. After all, even examiners are human; they warm to pieces of writing that intrigue, amuse, excite or argue coherently!

You should be able to write in a clear and logical manner. Your writing should reveal an ability to handle material and ideas at a sufficiently mature level. The content should be *relevant* to the topic you have chosen to write about.

Writing expressively is not just a matter of writing accurately and in correctly formed sentences, although accuracy is very important. Think about how *you* respond to things you read. A piece of writing either interests you or it doesn't. As far as you are concerned, it has something to say or it hasn't. The manner of its expression is lively or original or funny or charming or informative, or it isn't. An examiner or teacher assessing your writing will judge your efforts in the same ways. Does it hold the attention or is it dull? Is there anything fresh and original about it or is it mostly filling up the page with fairly meaningless words? You must put something of yourself into your writing.

Organisation

The content should be organised in a *structured manner* so that the reader can follow clearly the narrative, argument, description, statement, whatever it may be. Paragraph structure and the continuity of the writing will usually form part of the examiner's judgement of your ability to organise your material. In other words, clarity is very important. The person reading a piece of your writing must be able to see clearly how your thoughts or arguments are developing or where your story (narrative) is going. There must be a beginning, middle and end – preferably in that order! You must provide clear signposts for your reader.

Appropriateness of style

Your ability to use an appropriate tone and language, or *style*, for specific pieces of writing is an important factor in judging your performance in this section of the syllabus. Teachers and examiners talk about candidates having 'a sense of audience', i.e. the ability to suit the style they use for the purposes and the audience of particular pieces of writing.

This is particularly necessary for the more factual type of essay or piece of writing, but freer, more personal writing also requires an understanding of what is an appropriate style. The examiners are interested in assessing how well you can adopt a suitable tone and language for particular writing tasks. Having a sense of audience is important in Directed Writing as well.

Accuracy
Spelling! Punctuation! Grammar!
Of course, in any English exam or assessment of course work, you are going to be judged on:

> how accurately you can spell;
> how accurately you can punctuate;
> how grammatically correct your writing is.

Accuracy is an important element in all writing submitted in English course work or done under examination conditions.

The best candidates will be expected to spell correctly very common words and less common words. The best candidates will also show a good command of punctuation. In addition, those who are awarded high marks will follow grammatical conventions accurately and appropriately.

Sentence structure
Examiners will require you to construct sentences correctly and appropriately for particular contexts. You should be able to write using a variety of sentence constructions, not just (for example) in a monotonous succession of similarly constructed, short, simple sentences. The ability to write longer, more complex sentences – where they are appropriate – is a sign of a mature style.

Expression and vocabulary
How sure and wide-ranging are your powers of expression in written English? How extensive is your vocabulary? Can you use the language competently, imaginatively and appropriately in various writing modes? Examiners will be asking these questions when they judge your writing; you should be asking yourself the same questions.

You must aim to employ a wide vocabulary which is correctly used, shows some sensitivity and is appropriate to the context.

Marking
Some examination boards instruct their examiners to mark continuous writing on a 'general impression' basis, i.e. examiners have to take into account all the relevant aspects mentioned above – expression, accuracy, organisation, and so on – but without apportioning a specified part of the total mark to each aspect of the writing. Rather than, say, awarding 10/50 for expression, 10/50 for accuracy, and so on, examiners may be asked to give one overall mark out of the total mark for the unit, having considered all the relevant criteria.

Other boards may divide up the total mark available, apportioning a definite proportion of marks for various aspects of the writing, e.g. content, accuracy, syntax.

Whichever method of marking is used by the various examining groups, the criteria on which you will be judged in the writing sections of the syllabus, whether it is in the form of the course work or writing done in an exam, will be common to all the examining boards. You must:

> be aware of what those criteria are;
> pinpoint your own weaknesses in different techniques;
> practise those techniques and skills to improve your performance;
> transfer what you learn through practice to the writing you do in the examination itself or the course work you submit.

It is very often said that you cannot prepare yourself for a writing examination or improve your writing skills for your coursework folder. This is nonsense! In the pages that follow, you will learn how to acquire or improve the necessary skills and be given opportunities for relevant practice. 'Sample' answers will help you to pinpoint strengths and weaknesses.

If you absorb what is explained in these pages and adapt it to your individual needs, you will be in much better shape to face up to the writing sections of the English syllabus. You have to adopt as rigorous and detailed an approach to the technique of writing as you would to acquiring skills in any other subject, such as mathematics or geography. Don't leave it to chance or inspiration. Do something positive to improve your writing skills. The coursework element in the GCSE English exam is a golden opportunity for you to show a steady maturing and mastery of writing skills over a long period of time.

Exercise   Make a list of those aspects of your writing in order of 'weakness' which you realise you must work on to improve your performance, for example:

1   Organisation of material
2   Spelling
3   . . .

In the above example you would be stating that organisation is the weakest aspect of your writing, spelling the next major weakness, followed by the other weak points. Self-assessment is a useful way of pinpointing your weaknesses and working to overcome them.

Planning your continuous writing
You have to plan carefully what you are going to write in a piece of continuous writing. This is true whether you are writing it in an examination or for your coursework folder.

How to go about it
Here is a six-stage method of planning your writing:

1 Think about what you are going to write, having chosen your topic.
2 Jot down your first thoughts in brief note form.
3 Consider these first thoughts and then re-organise them, and any other ideas you have, into some kind of order.
4 Make a paragraph order, i.e. listing the main details in the order of paragraphs, creating a 'skeleton' or outline.
5 Write the piece.
6 Check it over carefully for inaccuracies or any small improvements you can make.

How long on planning?   In a writing examination how much time do you give to the planning stage? As a guideline, if you have an hour in which to write the piece, you can allow the first ten minutes for the first four stages of the planning method.

Checking   It is essential that you allow some time at the end for checking over what you have written. Check especially for spelling, punctuation, and grammatical errors.

Therefore, if you divide up the hour sensibly, the division of time among planning, writing and checking should come out like this:

If you have longer than an hour for the piece, then you would give slightly longer to each stage.

Dividing time between sections of the paper
If there are two parts to the Expression or Continuous Writing paper, do not make the fatal mistake of giving the first part, or the second part for that matter, the lion's share of the time. If you do this, then you will undoubtedly rush the writing of the second task and lose marks. Usually you are advised how long to spend on one part of a paper (e.g. 'You should spend an hour on this section.'). *Do not ignore this advice.* The marks

awarded to each section are also usually stated. There is no point in spending most of the time on a question where the maximum marks awarded are 30 and doing hardly anything for the second section which could be worth 20 marks. It is generally easier to pick up the first 5–10 rather than the last 5–10 marks in any section.

More about first thoughts   When you have decided from the range of writing suggestions open to you what you are going to write about, jot down your first thoughts as they come to you. Here are some 'first thoughts' notes on the topic 'The Excuse':

> games – young person hates them – excuse notes week after week – forged – suspicious teacher confronts pupil – solution

Ordering your thoughts   These first thoughts could then be re-arranged into a more organised order which can be used as the paragraph structure for the essay. This is the 'skeleton' or outline of your piece.

1   George hates compulsory games – winter cold; freezing in corner of sportsfield.
2   First excuse notes genuine from parents – then they refuse – decides to forge them.
3   Feelings of anxiety and guilt – arouses suspicions of games master.
4   Confronted by games master in tense cross-examination.
5   After a while confesses; PE master surprisingly sympathetic.
6   Parents informed of forging; consultation; indoor games option found for pupil.

When you are putting these first thoughts into order, consider the opening and closing paragraphs in particular. It is important to have a strong opening and an effective conclusion to your piece of writing.

Drafting and redrafting in course work

For continuous writing produced for coursework assessment, either in class time or at home, it is advisable to write a first draft which is a kind of practice run for the final version. You can share this first draft with your teacher and discuss how it can be improved. Then you write the final version which you submit for assessment. Note that this is not the same thing as submitting ordinary classwork writing for assessment, having your teacher correct it and then writing a fair copy which you re-submit. That is not allowed. Writing a first draft and then re-drafting it, however, is a part of the planning stage for writing continuous pieces for coursework.

Here are some titles you could be presented with either in the Expression paper or as part of the required course work, that would come into the category of personal writing:

1 Write about two separate occasions in your life when you had to make an important decision of some kind. On one of these occasions, you made what turned out to be a 'correct' decision; on the other the decision had less happy consequences.
2 'When I was . . .' Look back into your past and recall some events that have stayed vividly in your memory and which you consider to have helped to shape the kind of person you have become.
3 My favourite days of the year.
4 'He's a character!' or 'She's a character!' People often say that about interesting, unusual or eccentric individuals they know. Write about one or more 'characters' whom you have met.
5 Saturday night.
6 Myself in ten years' time.
7 The pursuit of happiness.

Each of these topics invites you to draw directly on your own experience or to reflect on past experience or something of personal importance. The last topic is a *reflective* essay, but as it involves the writer in expressing something personal, it can be considered under the same category. In personal writing you will be judged on how well you communicate personal experience and feelings to the reader.

Style
Because the subjects of this writing are 'personal', that does not mean to say that you can indulge in a wholly informal or colloquial style of writing. The best autobiographical and personal writing has a directness and an immediacy that invite readers to share the writer's experience. However, you must aim to do this without falling into the trap of being 'chatty' in your tone and language.

Writing is not the same as speaking. When you are writing a personal piece, you may well want to take your reader into your confidence, but writing can never be the same as chatting to your friends. Thus, you must find a style, a tone and a language which are appropriate to personal writing but which fall short of total informality or 'chattiness'.

To give you an example of the kind of 'matiness' to avoid, read this possible opening to an essay based on the first suggestion from the list above:

> Well, you could've knocked me down with a feather, I can tell you!
> What a decision! I've never made a worse one and I've made a few. Me

and my mates were going out for the evening and I decided to make up their minds about where we were going. Well, I would, wouldn't I?

That style could be acceptable if you were writing an essay 'in character', i.e. a story written in the first person using the words of a particular character who happens to talk in that manner. Then the chattiness of the tone emerges naturally from the fictional character you are using. If those words were part of a stretch of direct speech spoken by a character in a story, that too would be acceptable.

But as the opening to a piece of *personal* writing, it is too informal, too chatty, too colloquial. An improved opening that says more or less the same things would be:

> The consequences of my decision came as a shock, I must say. What a decision I had made! I've made some wrong choices in my life, but that was the worst.
>
> My friends and I were going out for the evening and I took it upon myself to decide where we were going. I admit that 'bossiness' is an occasional fault of mine!

The tone of the above is still fairly light and informal, which is appropriate for the topic, but a 'chatty' tone is avoided.

A further word of warning about style in personal essays: do not go to the other extreme and adopt a very formal tone and language in personal writing. Remember that your writing will be judged by how well you suit your style to the kind of writing you are attempting. To write a personal essay in such a colourless and impersonal style that the reader feels excluded from the experience being described is just as inappropriate as adopting too 'matey' a tone.

Advice about content

Obviously we cannot tell you what to write, but remember this: *you must try to interest your reader.*

Whatever subject you choose to write about in a piece of personal writing, ask yourself these questions:

> Is this likely to interest the reader or am I just filling up the page?
> Would I find this interesting if I were reading it?
> How can I make my experience more interesting to the reader?
> Am I keeping to the point and not just rambling on?

When you write about personal experience, you do not need to write about very dramatic or highly emotional incidents. As long as you make them seem important to you, and therefore interesting to your reader, the experiences you relate may be quite trivial in themselves.

Openings to personal writing

The opening to *any* piece of writing is very important.

You pick up a book: you read the first few paragraphs: usually you are either 'hooked' by then or you're not. In preparing to write a piece of personal writing, your task is the same as for any professional writer. You also have to interest the reader from the very first line.

Remember these useful rules:

1 *Do not pad your first paragraph with waffle just to get your writing started.* Consider your opening paragraph very carefully. When the examiner comes to weigh up your writing at the end and decide on a mark, he or she will certainly include as a factor the strength or weakness of the opening.
2 *Address the topic straight away.* In other words, do not have meaningless preambles or irrelevant introductions. If your subject is childhood memories, write about that topic from the first word. After all, your essay will consist only of between 400 and 600 words.
3 *Suit the style of your opening to the overall tone of your writing.* If you are going to write a thoughtful, reflective piece, you should set that tone in your first paragraph.

Sample openings

Refer back to the sample topics for personal writing we gave on page 28. Here are possible opening paragraphs for some of those topics.

1 *Good and bad decisions*
   I can well remember some of the 'good' and 'bad' decisions I have made in my life. The good or correct decision I remember most is one that led me to success in a field where I desperately wanted to be successful. The wrong-headed decision landed me in trouble that I could well have done without. One thing the making of these decisions taught me, however, was that you cannot make the right decisions all the time. Life has the habit of teaching you that lesson quite frequently, just in case you get too conceited and sure of yourself.

2 *Incidents from the past*
   Some incidents from your early life stay in your memory vividly, lighting up the past. A few intense experiences, some of which are important events in your life, others merely small incidents of no great significance, become forever imprinted in your memory, defining certain times in your existence. These experiences stand almost as symbols of the past in your mind. The 'symbolic' incidents I am going to tell you about will stay in my memory for the rest of my life. As I grow older, they may diminish in importance but I am sure I will never forget them.

3 *Favourite days of the year*
The first snowfall of the year. The first day of Spring. The beginning of the summer holidays. Hallowe'en. Christmas Day. These are a few of my favourite days of the year. Each has its own appeal. Each day brings its own special happiness. Each has its own flavour and atmosphere that you can almost touch.

4 *Characters*
Bertha is a large woman. Perhaps some would say she was fat, but they would not say it in her hearing. Bertha has her dignity and she is not to be insulted. I have seen Bertha defending herself against the insults of impertinent youths and, believe me, she can look after herself very well. That is one of the characteristics that make her one of the most interesting people I know.

5 *Saturday night*
Saturday seems a long way off from the vantage point of Monday morning. Saturday itself, of course, leads into Saturday night, the most exciting night of the week as far as I am concerned. But when Monday morning dawns, I never believe Saturday will ever come round again. I try to wish the hours and days away. Monday . . . Tuesday . . . by Wednesday I'm living on hope. Thursday I can believe. Friday, the eve of Saturday. And then Saturday comes in all its glory.

Ask yourself these questions about each of these openings:

Is it interesting? Does it grab your attention?
Does it engage the topic immediately?
Are the tone and language appropriate to the type of essay it is?
Does the opening paragraph introduce the topic well and make you want to read further?
Are there any faults you would comment on?

Exercise   Write interesting openings to each of the topics given on p. 18. In planning these openings consider the factors that are important to starting an essay of this type in an interesting and appropriate manner. Write well-developed opening paragraphs, not just one or two sentences. Pay special attention to the very first sentence.

Outlines and endings
We have already emphasised the need for planning your writing and creating skeleton outlines (see p. 25). Again we have to stress that you will not have long to prepare an outline in an examination, or during a timed piece in class for your course work, but it is important that you do one. It is just as important to plan your writing for untimed course work as well.

Practising outlines

Here are some more suggestions for topics.

1 Schooldays. Look back on the time you have spent at school. What have you gained from it? Have there been highs and lows, successes and failures, happiness and sadness? Write a piece summing up your feelings about your schooldays.

2 Surprise, surprise! Write about occasions in your life when you were taken by surprise by some events.

3 A few of my favourite things

4 The best holiday I ever had

Here is a possible outline for topic 1:

(*a*) Happiest days of your life? Hope not. Too many restrictions.

(*b*) Gained a lot; friendships, education, some amusing experiences; highs, lows, disappointments.

(*c*) Highs – winning the netball shield – appearing in school play.

(*d*) Lows – accident and long absence – trouble in the third year

(*e*) Happiness – friendships made – sadness – friendships lost.

(*f*) Conclusion – mixture of feelings, ambivalent about school – hope later life will be more consistently satisfying – rosy hue of memory.

Has this outline the promise of:

A definite, strong and direct opening paragraph?

Developed themes relevant to the topic?

A coherent development?

A definite conclusion?

Outline for topic 2:

(*a*) Surprises – sometimes great to be surprised – other times surprises can be nasty shocks; had my share of both varieties.

(*b*) Welcome surprises – won a competition in a magazine – couldn't believe it when letter arrived – thought they must have the wrong person – accepted prize gratefully.

(*c*) Other side of the coin – told by my doctor out of the blue I had illness which would take months to clear up – nasty jolt – made me value good health – envious of my friends during my illness.

(*d*) One school report – what a shock to me and my parents – made me determined to make them eat their words – nasty surprise worked to my benefit.

(*e*) Life a mixture of good and bad surprises – part of growing up to realise that – there will be more welcome surprises, more unwelcome – don't get carried away by good fortune or destroyed by bad.

Ask yourself the same questions about this outline as you did for the previous example.

Endings

In all writing, the way in which you end is just as important as your opening, and should be planned as part of the outline. A piece of personal writing should have a 'rounded-off' feel to it, so that the examiner sees that you have considered the structure of your essay and that you have had your reader very much in mind. Reflect on your own responses to reading. You probably think more highly of an article, report, story, or personal essay if it comes to a definite ending, rather than if it just breaks off very abruptly and leaves you, the reader, in mid-air.

One way of concluding an essay is by drawing the threads of what you have been writing about together and rounding it off with a concluding statement. Or you can sum up, in a different way, the gist of what you have been writing about. An alternative method, in personal writing, is to relate what you have been writing about to the reader's own experiences and perhaps leave him or her with some stimulating ideas to make him or her think about his or her own reactions.

Sample endings

Here is a sample ending or closing paragraph for topic 1:

> At present I have very mixed feelings about my experience of school. I have ambivalent views about the value of school anyway. My school-days have been useful at times and even happy occasionally, but there have been aspects of them that have been distinctly less rewarding. I only hope that I shall get more continuous satisfaction from my life in the future. No doubt many years from now, I will look back at my schooldays through the rosy hue of memory. They will provide some fond memories for my middle and old age. Perhaps I will even wax sentimental about them. You never know.

Sample ending to topic 2:

> There will always be surprises in life. They may come in the shape of nasty unpleasant shocks or delightful moments of unexpected joy. Life will have its share of both and it may be part of growing up to realise that. I suppose I will have to absorb the shocks and learn from them; I will relish the bonuses of luck and profit from them. Life is, after all, a continuous learning process.

Both these endings have the merit of sounding like closing paragraphs. They have the air of rounding things off, almost of summarising the writer's thoughts. They provide emphatic endings to both pieces.

Exercise Write outlines and closing paragraphs for topics 3 and 4 on page 31. In addition you could write outlines for 1 and 2. Consider the need for a coherent development, a strong opening, the relevance of the content, and a definite ending that is not too brief or hurried.

Marked example of 'personal' writing

Topic: 'Weekends'

The following essay has been marked. Errors have been picked out;
sometimes ticks indicate 'strengths'. A list of examiner's comments follows
the essay. Read the essay carefully and consider the examiner's comments.

My weekend starts imediately the pips go at a quarter to   sp.
four on a Friday afternoon. The weekend starts there
and doesn't end until my head hits the pillow on Sunday
night. My aim from four o'clock on Friday afternoon is
to make the most of the time that has been liberated for   √ vocab.
me. I quite like school but I like to have the weekend   repeti-
free to spend more or less as I like, parents willing.   tion

On that point, I have certain weekend responsibilities
which I must face up to for example I have to complete   pct.
any homework my teachers has set and take my share of   grammar
the household chores along with the rest of my family.
Apart from those two activities my time is my own and
do I try to make the most of it! On Monday mornings I
want to look back on the weekend and comfort myself
before the week begins again that I made the most of my
free time.

The campaign starts at around four on a Friday, as I   √ cont.
said. I rush home and phone up my friends. We might
already have a good idea of what we're going to do on a
Friday evening, but it's pleasant anyway to talk over
things and gosip about the passed weak. We might   sp. × 3
decide to go to a disco at the club or to the local pictures.
Occasionally we meet up at one of our houses to watch a
video film or play records. That takes care of Friday!

Saturday begins usually with chores.   para.

There's no avoiding my share but everyone pitches in
so there is no ill-will about doing the shopping, cleaning
the flat and washing the car. Mowing the lawn in   sent.
summer.   constr.

On Saturday afternoons I often go and watch the local
football team, the Nightingales. At the match I shout my
head of until I'm hoarse. The Nightingales are going   sp.
through a bad season and so I haven't had much to cheer
about lately. I do not allow the result of the match to
spoil my Saturday evening, the peak of my week!

If we haven't been to a disco on the Friday evening, we
(my two friends and me) make doubly sure that we go   grammar
dancing on Saturday evening. There are three clubs in
the vicinity that we favour with our presence. There is a   √ vocab.
succession of Saturdays when we go to one of the three,
then we get tired of that place and go to one of the other

two the next week. We dance the night away and the only aspect of the evening that can spoil our enjoyment is if some 'yobs' cause trouble. Fortunately, that is a rare ocurrence.

√ vocab.
√ pct.
sp.

Sunday morning is a time for a lie-in! I stumble through for 'brunch' at about midday and cast a cursory eye over the Sunday newspapers. In the afternoon I do some homework and then I usually watch a film that I have recorded previously.

√ vocab.

Sunday evening is usually fairly relaxing. I sometimes visit a friend's or relative's house, or meet friends in a local café to chat and have some fun. By the time ten o'clock comes round I'm feeling quite exhausted and I go none too reluctantly to bed at about 10.30.

√ vocab.

That, then is the shape of most of my weekends. I expect nobody would consider it exceptionally exciting fare but I value my weekends greatly and as long as they give me satisfaction, that is all that really matters. I obviously set some store by my weekends because immediately the week begins, I'm looking forward to the next weekend. My mother warns me against wishing my life away, but I can't resist it. I have to have something to look forward to!

√ cont.

Examiner's comments:
Length: well above minimum length.
Content: relevant; lively approach to topic and communicates enthusiasm; gives details of weekends.
Organisation: has a reasonably direct and strong opening. Definite structure to the essay and logical sequence; last paragraph rounds it off. One paragraph consists of one sentence only for no apparent reason, however.
Expression: appropriate tone and language; light touch without being too chatty or colloquial. Some above average vocabulary.
Accuracy: spelling errors, mostly careless and avoidable.
Grammatical errors: subject-verb agreements: 'me' instead of 'I'.
Punctuation: two errors but generally sound.
Sentence construction: excellent command of sentence structure and a variety of lengths. One non-sentence, however.
Summary: generally, a well-written essay, organised, interesting, communicating personal response to topic. The mechanical errors, especially the spelling errors, spoil it to a degree, but they do not hinder effective communication.

Having read through the essay and the examiner's comments carefully, correct any errors that have been pointed out. Are there any other comments you would add to the examiner's remarks?

Unmarked example of 'personal' writing
On the next two pages there is another 'personal' piece of writing, this time on the topic 'Friends'. This piece has been left unmarked and no examiner's comments have been added. Put yourself in the place of the examiner. Read through the piece carefully, marking any mechanical errors of spelling, grammar, punctuation and sentence construction (for corrections see p. 176). Consider the structure of the piece. Does it have a strong opening; is it logically and clearly developed; is the continuity between paragraphs effective; is the paragraph structure sound? What do you think of the expression, range of vocabulary and sentence construction? Is the content interesting, and is the essay rounded off neatly and satisfactorily? How would you rate it overall as a piece of writing: excellent, very good, good, average, quite poor, very poor?

Friends

Friendship is one of the most valuable things in life. Without freinds we can feel very much alone in a thretening world. Friends can come to our rescue, console us, make us laugh, keep us company, drive us mad and generally enliven our lives. A person without friends has to face up to life's inevitable troubles alone and that is a daunting prospect.

However, friends can bring drawbacks with them. Who hasnt been let down by a friend. Friends can disappoint and annoy us. They can break their promises, forget to pay you back the money they owe, grate on your nerves in so many ways, they can be to inquisitive or too distant, they can have irritating habits such as telling the same boring 10 jokes all the time or singing tunelessly when you are trying to concentrate on something. In fact, friends are individuals with their attractive *and* their less appealing features. Everyone has their faults.

Some people are called 'fair weather friends'. This means they are only friends if things are going well for you. The minute you need help or are in some kind of trouble, they disappear. If you have ever been in need of real consolation or help, then you will have discovered who your real friends are. They will be the once who stick by you, offering aid and comfort, supporting you through the bad times and sacrificing things for your sake. The 'fair weather friends' will have meanwhile 20 vanished into the night.

Times of sadness or misfortune can, then, bring the benefit that you find out who your real friends are, happy times are obviously less of a strain on friendships but even then, each party to a friendship has to work at it to make it endure. As in a marriage there has to be a 'give-and-take' prosess. People always compete with one another, even friends. They have different needs and goals. Real friends will recognise one another's rights and take steps to make sure they are accommodated within the friendship. One friend cannot always ' dominate in a friendship; that is not particularly healthy and will 30 almost inevitably lead to a quarrel. Genuine friendship involves the recognition of each other's individuality whilst preserving a bond that unites and supports both parties.

Yet it is seldom that easy to find a friendship that will last. Indeed not all friendships need endure. After all, you can be friends with people for the duration of something you are sharing – schooldays, a holiday, neighbours – and not continue the friendship after what have brought you together has ended. Friendships are very ofetn based on a shared interest for a period and then people naturally go their own ways.
40   There is no real need for regret on that score.

However, when you do find a friend that you know will be important in your life, then you must recognise the fact and do all in your power to keep the friendship intact.

Cynics might say that the basis of all friendship is 'scratch my back and I'll scratch yours'. In other words, mutual self-interest dictates whom we choose as friends. There may, after all, be a grain of truth in that. Friendships are often formed through necessity, because individuals can help each other, or even profit in numerous ways from being friends. But real friendship transcends any idea of knowing
50   people simply because the friendship can do you some good. True friends want the best for one another, regardless of any benefit that might come their way. However, not all friends truly wish each other well. Who was it who said that there was nothing harder to bear than the news of the success of a friend?

But friendships are to be treasured and cosseted. They bring warmth and security to your life. People need other people. I confess it quiet openly, I need my friends. Friends rid my life of the spectre of loneliness. Family is the other consoling blanket in life, but relatives are not always enough, in my experience. You need to have people you
60   care about and who care about you, outside the family circle. Long live friendship!

More topics
1   'That really irritates me!' Write an essay about the small things that irritate you when they happen.
2   Write about some pleasures that bring you great satisfaction or contentment.
3   'That's my idea of a perfect day!' What is your idea of a 'perfect day'?
4   My very first memories
5   Part-time jobs. Describe any part-time job(s) you have had, making clear why you found them satisfying, or otherwise, to do.
6   Loneliness
7   'My ambitions are to . . .' Write an essay explaining what some of your ambitions for the future are.
8   Going abroad: what do you like and dislike about going abroad?

Argumentative writing is sometimes referred to as 'discursive' writing, 'discussion', or even 'opinion essays'. These terms cover the types of writing in which you have to argue a point of view and express your opinions about an issue of importance or a statement that is presented to you and to which you are asked to react.

Possible topics

1 'Young people nowadays are just as willing to commit themselves to improving society and helping other people as they have ever been.' Discuss this statement in a piece of continuous writing.

2 Argue the case for or against the banning of all cigarette smoking in public places, e.g. cinemas, buses, trains, workplaces.

3 'The criminal nowadays is dealt with far too leniently. Much more consideration should be given to the victims of crime.' Discuss both these statements, making clear what your opinions are.

4 Some people have argued that every adult should be paid a 'social wage' by the State which would be enough to pay for the costs of basic living. Money earned by working would be additional to this 'social wage'. What do you think of this idea?

Personal response

In a sense, argumentative writing is a branch of personal writing. You are, after all, responding with your own opinions and expressing something important about yourself. But the argumentative piece requires a specific approach and different techniques from personal writing. Argumentative writing must be carefully planned, structured and expressed, and usually requires a certain level of maturity on the part of the candidate.

What writing skills do you need?

If you write an argumentative piece in an English exam or as a 'timed' assignment in class or for your coursework folder you must be able to:

argue a case clearly and logically;

have sufficient interest in the topic to sustain the interest of the reader through a long piece;

structure the writing so that there is a development of ideas from the opening paragraph to a definite conclusion – continuity;

adopt an appropriate style that avoids sweeping generalisations and wild exaggerations;

provide a balanced appraisal of conflicting arguments while expressing your own opinions as well.

Continuity

We have already stressed the need for continuity in writing. In argumentative pieces continuity is of extra importance. Your paragraphs should follow on naturally by using linking words or phrases, or some reference to points made in the previous paragraph, to develop a coherent argument.

Here are some phrases that can be useful in linking together points in an argumentative piece if they are placed at the beginning of paragraphs:

> Another argument often used is . . .
> Those who oppose this point of view argue that . . .
> The logical conclusion of that argument is . . .
> However, my own point of view is . . .
> It could be argued that . . .
> On the other hand . . .
> In support of this argument . . .
> An additional argument for this point of view is . . .
> A strong case can also be made for . . .
> Another point that must be considered is . . .

To illustrate the use of linking words and phrases between paragraphs, read these three paragraphs as a sample opening on topic 3 on page 38.

> The problem of how best to punish violent criminals and to compensate the innocent victims of their crimes is not open to easy solution. Sweeping statements like those in this question are not particularly helpful. They are emotional, biased and totally ignore the root causes of crime.
>
> There are those who argue that crime is always caused by naturally wicked people. I do not believe this to be true. There are very real reasons – poverty, ignorance, chronic unemployment – why most criminals turn to crime.
>
> However, it is undoubtedly true that the amount of violent crime has risen dramatically over the last twenty years. I would argue that this is because society itself has become much more violent.

The first paragraph ends by referring to 'the root causes of crime'. This subject is continued in the second paragraph and is introduced by 'There are those who argue that . . .', which provides a bridge between the paragraphs. The word 'However' does the same for the second and third paragraphs, helping to introduce an opposing argument at the beginning of the third paragraph.

Exercise   Consider the range of issues and topics that could be set as topics for argumentative essays. Make a list of possible topics. Having done that, decide which of these topics you think you could deal with competently and persuasively in an argumentative essay.

Planning argumentative writing

Argumentative pieces may need slightly different planning techniques from other types of continuous writing because of the nature of the task. You should try to provide a balanced view of an issue. That does not mean you have to suppress your own feelings and opinions. On the contrary, the purpose of an argumentative expression is to allow you to voice those opinions and to argue a case you believe in, but you must also deal with the arguments opposed to your point of view. This involves balancing the scales of argument and then coming down either on one side or the other, with your reasons, or recognising that there are valid points on both sides.

Balancing the argument

In your initial planning notes, it is very useful to make two lists of opposing arguments: 'For' and 'Against'. We will now do that for topic 1 on page 38: 'Young people nowadays are just as willing to commit themselves to improving society and helping other people as they have ever been.'

For	*Against*
In own experience lots of young people do voluntary work	Destructive urges: vandalism, hooliganism, rising crime figures
Give specific examples of young people helping old people	'I'm all right, Jack' attitude
Youthful idealism also channelled into political action; campaigns, demonstrations, religious beliefs.	Disaffected youth wasting time
	Aimless pursuits, e.g. television, video games, amusement arcades
Adult cynicism usually projected on to young people, leading to unfair generalisations	Drug-taking
	Level of violence and alienation among young people

Outline

(*a*) Introduction: address topic of youthful willingness to try and serve community; make clear own point of view.

(*b*) Own experience of community service; helping old people; raising funds for charitable causes; counter argument that all young people involved in football hooliganism and rioting.

(*c*) Idealism vs. cynicism; hard to hold on to youthful enthusiasm if crushed by unemployment, but many young people involved in supporting causes, political movements, etc.; concern for minority rights; contrary to notion that 'I'm all right Jack' attitude prevails.

(*d*) More examples of youthful idealism: work to help handicapped and children; every generation complains about young – has little real meaning.

(*e*)   Argument about drug-taking and glue-sniffing – each generation has found its own channel of rebellion – in fifties, teddy boys; sixties, hippies; eighties, youth rebellion against adult indifference.

(*f*)   On balance, young are committed to helping; must be given encouragement, channel their energies into useful actions; no point in blanket disapproval; ideals of young generation will shape future society.

Another outline

Here are possible 'For' and 'Against' lists for topic 2 listed on page 37: 'Argue the case for and against the banning of all cigarette smoking in public places, e.g. cinemas, buses, trains, workplaces.'

For	*Against*
Smoking great danger to individual/public health	Smoking matter of personal freedom
Even non-smokers suffer from 'passive' smoking	People against smoking are selfish
Non-smokers need to be more forceful about their rights	Individual freedoms gradually cut down in this country
Personal freedoms dependent on doing harm to other people	Amount of smoke non-smokers inhale is minimal
Medical evidence shows that non-smokers can get lung cancer from cigarette smoke around them	Mere propaganda by anti-smoking pressure groups

(*a*)   Agree with banning; smoking is huge danger to individual and public health.

(*b*)   Non-smokers affected in public places; forced to inhale smokers' smoke; in own home should request smokers not to smoke; it's smokers who are selfish.

(*c*)   Non-smokers need to assert their rights to breathe clean air; not a matter of individual freedom; freedom to pollute?

(*d*)   One man's freedom can be another man's loss; not free to do harm to other people; free to harm their own health, not other people's.

(*e*)   Argument that non-smokers only inhale tiny amounts of smoke not valid; medical evidence shows non-smokers can get lung cancer through inhaling cigarette smoke.

(*f*)   Not just propaganda; real health risk; evidence cannot be ignored; dirty unsocial habit; only fools and selfish people would do it.

Exercise   Draw up 'For' and 'Against' lists for topic 3 on page 38. You should include at least six arguments on both sides. Having done that, write detailed outlines for one or both of these essays, based on your lists.

Openings to argumentative or discussion writing

Each type of sustained writing needs a strong opening and a definite conclusion, but obviously different kinds of opening (and concluding) paragraphs are required for argumentative discussion pieces and personal or narrative writing.

Openings

The topics for argumentative discussion writing are often in the form of a statement which you are expected to discuss and give your opinions about. Or you are asked a question about an issue and your piece is meant to be a response to the question. However the topic is worded, your first paragraph must make direct reference to the topic under discussion.

Consider this topic:

> 'Women's place is in the home.' Discuss this well-known saying, making clear your own views about women's role in modern society.

Here is a possible opening paragraph written in response to that topic:

> I could not agree less with the sentiment that the role of women is restricted to the domestic scene. Women have just as much right as men to develop their interests and involvements in every sphere of life. Changes in modern society would seem to support my view, as we can easily see that women are no longer restricted to the roles of wife and mother. The role of women can never again be restricted in society as it has been in the past.

In the first sentence, the writer's attitude to the statement is made clear and, at the same time, the topic is itself mentioned or addressed. The three other sentences introduce the ideas of women's right to develop outside the home and women's changing role in modern society. Clearly, these points are going to be developed further in the writing. The *strengths* of this opening are:

> it addresses the topic immediately;
> it makes clear the writer's point of view;
> it makes points that can be developed later;
> the style is clear and direct.

Consider this topic:

> 'Money is the root of all evil.' Discuss this statement in an essay.

Below is a possible opening:

> Money can certainly have good and evil influences on people. It is a commodity we all have to deal with, but our attitudes to it vary considerably. Some people seem largely indifferent to it, others spend their entire energies acquiring it. I fall somewhere in the middle. I do

not think money is the root of all evil, although undoubtedly it is the cause of some.

Ask yourself these questions about this opening:

Does it address the topic immediately?
Does it introduce aspects of the topic that can be developed later?
Is the writer's own attitude to the topic made clear?

Consider also this topic:

'In a time of very serious unemployment, married women should be encouraged not to take jobs but to stay in the home.' Discuss this statement making clear what your own opinions are.

Here is a possible opening paragraph:

I could not agree less with the opinion expressed in the statement. Men and women should have absolutely equal rights and opportunities to take full-time jobs and further their careers whatever their personal circumstances. This statement seems to advocate that the role of women, especially married women, should be limited to the home. I hope those days of limiting what women can do with their lives are gone forever. Those women who choose to be housewives should, of course, be entirely free to do so, but for the many others who want a role outside the home, opportunities for careers and full-time jobs should be as freely available as they are to men.

The first sentence makes the opinion of the writer quite clear. This is followed up by an equally clear expression of belief in equality of opportunity for men and women. These two sentences get the discussion off to an emphatic start. However, the tone is firm, not sweeping. The paragraph continues with development of the point about equal opportunities and it also refers to the 'house-bound' role of women, as mentioned in the question.

Exercise Practise writing opening paragraphs to any of the topics mentioned in this section. Or, if you prefer, write the opening paragraphs based on the following:

1 There have been moves recently to re-introduce capital punishment for certain serious crimes. What are your views about this issue?
2 'Newspapers nowadays are more like comics or light-hearted magazines. They should be more serious and informative.' Discuss this statement in a piece of continuous writing.
3 Many people, especially many women, object to beauty contests. They say such contests demean women in general. Do you agree or disagree?

Endings to argumentative writing

Clearly, the conclusion to an argumentative piece is also very important. You cannot leave the argument 'hanging in mid-air'. You cannot leave your reader with the dissatisfied feeling that the case for a particular point of view has been left in an unfinished state. You must draw an argumentative piece to a definite conclusion.

Let us go back to the topics on pages 42–3 for which we wrote opening paragraphs. Here is a possible concluding paragraph on 'women's place':

> Finally, it has to be said that individual women will continue to make their own choices about the kind of life they want to lead. Some women will perceive their role as being wife and mother for most of their lives. Many others will try to combine these roles with the responsibility of earning a living or having a career. Many will choose to devote themselves to a career and not get married and have children. The important issue, to my mind, is that those choices should be open to all women for them to be able to make a decision for themselves. In the past, women's place has had to be in the home because no other real choice existed.

Note these points about that concluding paragraph:

> The use of 'finally' at the start of the paragraph *signals* that the piece is coming to an end and that the writer is summarising the arguments.
> It discusses the various choices open to women in the future.
> It re-states the writer's position in the sentence beginning 'The important issue, to my mind, is . . .'.
> The final sentence refers again to the topic ('women's place is in the home') and makes a concluding statement about it.

Read this possible concluding paragraph on 'money':

> Money, then, brings out ambivalent attitudes in me. I want as much money as I can get as long as I earn it in an acceptable and enjoyable manner. But I do see signs around me in society that money has become the god of many people. I dislike the fact that money can buy you extra privileges and can even mean the difference between life and death, as I have pointed out in my discussion about health care. Money is certainly not the root of all evil, but evil things are caused by our greed for it. The solution is that everyone should have a fairer share of the money that is available in our society.

Ask yourself these questions about this concluding paragraph:

> Does the writer use a word, or words, that could alert the reader that the piece is coming to an end?
> Does it seem to sum up some of the points the writer has been making in the piece?

Does it 'address', or refer to, the statement that candidates had to use
for the starting-point of the piece?
Does the final sentence make a definite concluding statement?
Is the writer's opinion about the subject clearly expressed?

Read this possible concluding paragraph for the topic on women and jobs
from the previous section:

I feel strongly on this issue. When times are bad and there is an
economic recession, the claims that men have more right to employment than women are always heard, but if women are ever to progress
to total equality, they will have to counter that kind of argument and
resist such strong social pressures. Women have for a long time now
been told to be patient and that change is gradual, that the time is not
'ripe' at the moment. When will that 'ripe' time come? The answer
must be now, here in the present. Women must push for their rights,
not be fobbed off by male excuses. Most women now see through those
excuses and are no longer content to accept them meekly.

Ask yourself these questions about this concluding paragraph:

How does the first sentence of the paragraph make an effective
opening to a concluding paragraph?
What is there about the tone of the paragraph that makes it sound like
it is summing up the arguments?
Is the last sentence an effective way of ending the discussion?

In the concluding paragraph of a discussion piece, you need not take a
definite point of view on an issue, coming down on one side or the other. If
you have been taking a 'balanced' view throughout the writing, pointing to
the strength of one side's arguments and the strengths of the counter-
arguments, you can keep to that balanced view in the final paragraph. Here
is a sample closing paragraph of this kind:

As I have indicated, I can see merits in both sides of the argument.
Married women, like all women, have every right to take up full-time
employment. In times of mass unemployment, however, is there not a
case for married people, men and women agreeing that only one of
them should be in employment? It could be the male partner who
remains at home and the woman who goes to work. In this way
unemployment could be shared more fairly across the population. I
can see, however, how this would upset many people as well. The only
real solution is to provide employment opportunities for everyone.

Exercise Write a concluding paragraph to pieces on any of the above
topics. Or, if you prefer, write the concluding paragraphs of writing based
on the topics listed on page 43, i.e., capital punishment, newspapers or
beauty contests.

Marked example of argumentative writing

Here is a marked example of an argumentative piece on the topic 'Many people, especially many women, object to beauty contests. They say such contests demean women in general. Do you agree or disagree?'.

I agree that beauty contests do tend to demean women. People should not be judged more or less like cattle. Beauty contests turn women into objects to be judged according to stereotyped images of what female beauty is supposed to be. Although I would not go as far as to ban beauty contests, I think they should be discouraged. For example, there should be no television screening of such events.

The defenders of these events clam that they are quite sp.
harmless, they dismiss the critics of beauty contests as pct.
extreme bigots who, because they do not excell in the sp.
beauty steaks themselves, frown upon any woman gain- sp.
ing fame and money threw making the most of her looks. sp.
These people fail to understand that these contests are
highly exploitative and harmful to the cause of women's √ vocab.
equality. Women is now just managing to escape from grammar
the straitjacket that men has created for them. Beauty grammar
contests put their advancement back by years.

Imagine if there were beauty contests for men! What would most most sensitive and intelligent men think of a competition that asked contestants to parade in brief costumes in front of a female panel and be assessed by the yardstick of how close they came to some stereo-typed image of male attractiveness? I would imagine many men would find such a practice ridiculous and offensive. They would find it even more offensive if they themselves began to be judged in ordinary life by the standards applied in such beauty contests with their emphasis wholly on physical characteristics. Men would not want to be categorised and imprisoned by a female dictate that said 'You will look like this and behave in this way!'

Men who support the idea of beauty contests as 'harmless' are almost the worst kind of male chauvinist. They like to think of women either as decorative, but mindless, sexual objects or as wives and mothers whose main role in life is to serve them, the dominant males, and their children. Women who are willing to parade themselves in beauty contests are accepting the role that men want women to play in society. They help the cause of male chauvinism because they pose no threat to male supremacy.

Why then do women continue to enter these contests? Many are dazzled by the promise of fame and glamour, and the large cash prizes. But there goals are mainly   sp. illusions; very few women win fame and fortune through beauty contests. The people who make the real money are the men who exploit the women by putting on these contests in the first place. As usual, men, becos of their   sp. power in society are able to exploit women and make profits from their efforts.

However, beauty contests have more important and lasting effects. They set up images of women that influence girls. They teach them that the way to be valued is to come as near to looking like the beauty queens as possible. Men are not subjected to the same kind of   √ vocab. pressure and we would soon hear them squeal if they were. Young people of both sexes have their understanding of the relationship between the sexes re-   √ vocab. inforced by such events. Women are seen as having to measure up to men's fantasies about them.

You do not have to be an ardent feminist to object to beauty contests. More and more people are beginning to realise that beauty contests are like cattle shows. It may take some time for them to disappear entirely, but the signs are that they will in time. One good sign is that the BBC have decided not to show any more of these events. Publicity is vital to these contests because finally they are all about making money for a few people. The contestants themselves are used for a short while, then cast aside. Perhaps soon we will be in a position where no contests can take place because no woman will enter. When we reach that stage, women will have gained full equality.

Examiner's comments:
Content: relevant; mature approach to topic; makes points strongly and deals with some opposing arguments.
Organisation: direct opening paragraph, making own opinion quite clear. Logical development of ideas and linking of paragraphs. Linking words/ phrases used: 'the defenders of *such* events' – 'such' refers back to first paragraph. Fifth paragraph: 'Why *then* do such women . . .'. The final paragraph sums up arguments; last sentence rounds off the piece effectively.
Expression: firm, forceful style but avoids going over the top in sweeping generalisations. Strongly held views but style is controlled. Above average vocabulary: 'exploitative', 'subjected to', 'reinforced by'.
Accuracy: careless spelling errors and some poor sentence construction.
Grammar: subject–verb agreements.
Summary: a well-argued essay.

Unmarked example of argumentative writing
Once again put yourself in the place of an examiner reading and marking the essay below. There are numerous errors which you should detect and correct (see p. 176). Ask yourself questions about the content, organisation, expression and range of vocabulary; write comments on the piece. The topic is: 'Newspapers nowadays are more like comics or light-hearted magazines. They should be more serious and informative.' What are your opinions of today's newspapers?

The standard of poplar journalism in this country is generally thought to have declined over the last ten years. Not so long ago newspapers like the Daily Mirror, although catering for a mass readership, seemed to try and inform their readership about important issues. Now the mass circulation papers seem more interested in selling their bingo games.

What has caused this decline in newspaper standards? I agree that the kind of journalism we read in these papers like the 'Sun', 'Mail' and 'Mirror' is terribly poor. The battle for readers and the big money that can be made from running a large national newspaper has a lot to do   10
with the decline. It seams that newspapers now cater for the lowest common denominator and try to appeal to the basest feelings of their readers. They concentrate almost entirely on the most sensational and lurid stories and when there is know hard news, reporters invent storeys, sometimes harming innocent reputations in the process.

People now tend to expect very little from their newspapers, or at least from the so-called tabloid press. Television gives them most of the information they want about the world. Most people seem to prefer seeing pictures about events rather than reading about them in depth. This helps to create a very ill-informed electorate.   20

Even when the tabloid press turns to 'serious' matters, they will inevitably trivialise the issues by concentrating on personalities or side issues which they think their readers will be more interested in. Everything seems to come down to its value as 'entertainment'. Newspaper proprietors and editors seem to think that readers will shy away from anything that smacks of real analysis or information. Trivial articles, sport, gossip and scandal – that is the staple diet offered to most newspaper readers. The defenders of the popular press points to the huge readership that the most mindless newspapers acquire and argue that they are only giving the public exactly what they want. If   30
that is true, then the education of the public has been sadly neglected. If the general public were judged by the standards of the yellow press, then you would be forced to the conclusion that the majority are semi-literate, entirely frivolous and full of the worst prejudices.

The political attitudes of many newspapers reveal a good deal of bias. They make little attempt to present a balanced view of things.

Opinions masquerade as fact and the readership are prejudiced against the people, parties and causes the particular newspaper is out to destroy.

40 Because newspapers are more like comics, important issues are turned into trivia by writers who are told not to stretch the brain cells of the readers too much. This would be harmless if you believed that people's opinions are not partly formed by what they read in their newspapers. There is a good deal of evidence, however, that people do get many of their opinions from what they read. The danger is that our socity will turn into a semi-literate one in which politicians and other people with things to sell will able to fool a mass audience because they have been fed with trivia and a total lack of real analysis for years.

One of the functions of a free press is to turn the searchlight on 50 governments and officials of all kinds and to expose corruption, stupidity and injustice. Today's tabloids are far more interested in exposing the charms of pin-up girls. They pander to the prejudices and lowest instincts of their readership. They write about rock and film stars, the private lives of royalty; they print the confessions of notorious people and dwell on the seamy side of life.

What can be done, then, to improve this situation? To start and continue printing a newspaper intended for a mass readership costs millions of pounds. It is unlikely that many newspapers will be born in the next ten or twenty years. The answer really lies in the readers 60 themselves. They have to stop buying papers that insult their intelligence with trivia and sensational nonsense. But if most of the readers are satisfied with what they read, what hope is there? I think schools should help young people to analyse the content of newspapers and expose the sensational and mindless approaches of the tabloid press. If the next generation demands more of their newspapers, then there would be much less chance of 'comic' papers continuing to exist and making the vast profits they do at present.

More topics for argumentative/discussion writing

1 'The right to strike is one of our most precious freedoms.' Discuss this statement.

2 Discuss the arguments for and against Britain having nuclear weapons, making clear in your writing what your own views are.

3 'Everyone should earn more or less the same wages, then there would be less conflict and dissatisfaction in our society.' Discuss this statement.

4 Do you think the 'pop' music business exploits young people by persuading them to spend so much money on records and tapes?

5 'Scientific experiments on animals should not be allowed, whatever the benefit to mankind.' Discuss this statement.

Narrative is telling a story or giving an account of something.

Some candidates choose a narrative topic in an English exam or for course work because they think it is an easy option. This is definitely not so!

Telling a story in a manner that holds the attention of the reader is a skilled technique. We can all tell a story badly. In your narrative writing for your coursework folder and in an exam, you must aim to produce concisely written, tightly structured story-telling.

The technique

Let's make the comparison between telling a story and telling a joke. We have all heard people trying to tell a joke and making an absolute mess of it, so that the joke falls flat and no one laughs. The same joke, however, when told by someone who is aware of such matters as timing, pace, clarity, emphasis and delivery, can lead to people falling about with laughter. 'It's the way I tell them,' says one popular comedian. Well, it's the way you tell your stories, too, that counts.

The ideas for your stories

We all probably see many television series and films. It is a sad fact that far too many candidates in English examinations and in their course work rehash something they have seen on television or in a film. It is usually very obvious and most of the plots they use are very unsuitable anyway.

Golden rule: do not regurgitate the plots of films or television series!

Another 'don't' is to write a story that takes the reader through a very elaborate plot and then announce at the end: 'Suddenly I jolted up in bed, the sweat standing out on my forehead. It had all been an awful dream!'

You may think this is a highly original ending, but, believe me, 'it was all a dream, after all' endings are very common and examiners get heartily sick of them. They are very clichéd.

Content

The restriction of length and time is very important in writing a narrative piece. What you are really being asked to do is write a short story; in fact, a 'short' short story.

If you try to cram too much into the short story, it will appear overblown and shapeless. You have to choose a *storyline* that can be adequately told within the limitations imposed by the length you are expected to write. You also have to allow for some dialogue and some description. Perhaps you might want to include some reflections on the story.

You do *not* want your story to be very bare narrative of this type:

He walked across the busy main road. Then he turned right. He stopped outside a house. Then he climbed the stairs to the first floor. He then rang the bell. The door opened and then he went in.

Think of your reader. Would the reader really be interested in this kind of plodding, repetitive story-telling? The 'Then he . . .' construction should be used very seldom. If there are too many 'Then he . . .' constructions in your story it is almost certainly because the plot is too complicated for the length of the story or because you are dwelling on unimportant narrative detail. You must select carefully what you include in your narrative. Every detail and action described must be important to the story.

Part of the art of effective story-telling is to include in your stories:

description   direct speech   characterisation

Obviously in a short story you cannot include a great deal of description, but *brief vivid details* of how people, things and places look and how people behave add to the impact of a story.

Direct speech is often a more effective way of carrying on a story than narrative. The actual words people say can tell you a great deal about them as individuals and about the situation they are in.

Characterisation is not separate from direct speech, description and narrative. Characterisation is about giving an *individuality* to the people in your stories, making them stand out as real people.

Structure of stories

The telling of the story, the narrative, must be pacy but must not be rushed. The narrative must not drag but it must not go so fast that the story becomes jumbled and loses all impact.

Exercise   Go to a library and find some anthologies of short stories. Read as many short stories as you have time for. Consider each of them from these points of view:

Theme: what is it about?

Structure: does it have a definite shape to it – a beginning, middle and an end? Or is it more the type of short story that is atmospheric with really very little plot?

Opening: how did the writer try to grab your attention from the very first line?

Description: were there any brief descriptions that added to your enjoyment of the stories?

Direct speech: how much of it was there and how was it used?

Characterisation: did you get a real idea of the characters?

Ending: was it a surprise ending? Did the story satisfy you as a reader?

Story-telling: all in all, did the writer tell the story in an interesting way and keep to the point?

List the short stories you read and give them a rating from 1 to 10.

Opening your story

The best advice we can give is to involve your reader immediately in the story. You simply cannot afford long preambles that are mainly page-filling and largely irrelevant to the main story, as in this example where the candidate is writing an adventure story, the main character being a fairly ordinary young person:

> I got up at the usual time. I threw back the covers, stretched, waited my turn for the bathroom and then went downstairs for breakfast. For breakfast I always had two eggs, bacon and sausages.
>
> 'Hello, Mum. Hello, Dad,' I said.
>
> 'Hello, son,' said my mother. 'Get a move on, you'll be late.'
>
> 'He's always late,' moaned Dad, disappearing as usual behind the newspaper.

This opening might be acceptable if you were describing a typical early morning scene in your home, but if your subject is an adventure that happens later in the day, then what the character had for breakfast that day and what he said to his Mum and Dad at the breakfast table are entirely irrelevant. In a short story you have to *select the narrative detail carefully*. The above example will not grab the reader's attention and illustrates what you should *not* do.

If you are to avoid irritating preambles, then what kind of opening should you aim for? There are various types of openings to stories; you should try to suit the type of opening you use to the kind of story you are writing.

The 'wham-bam' opening

> The bomb exploded and all hell was let loose. People ran screaming round the square terrified out of their minds. I stumbled among the debris, the sound of the explosion still roaring in my head.

This kind of opening plunges the reader straight into the action with something dramatic happening in the first paragraph or even the first sentence. But beware – do not attempt to keep your story at this pitch all the way through by piling incident upon incident. Allow for a variation in pace. Add description and direct speech. Build some characterisation.

The atmospheric opening

> The wood echoed with the cries of solitary birds and animals. Through the leaves of the tall trees the sun's beams radiated their warmth. She sat against the trunk of an ancient oak tree. A ladybird ran elegantly up her bronzed arm. She sighed. Everything seemed to be at peace.

This is a gentle opening; the scene is being set. The writer is trying to create a mood, an atmosphere. The writer can then choose to continue the atmosphere in the narrative or shatter it completely by something unexpected or unpleasant happening.

The brisk, direct narrative approach
It was a Tuesday. George was coming home from work at the same time he always did. He crossed the street at the library and nodded to Mr Greenaway, the grocer at the corner shop. Suddenly, a voice hailed him from behind.

This opening has the virtue of immediately introducing the main character, the setting and first incident of the story. It more or less plunges straight into the story but without the sensational start of the 'wham-bam' opening.

The unusual opening
Zoltan noticed that the household pet was winding down. The dog's movements had become uncertain and his barking muffled. This was a sure sign that his five-year battery was running down. Zoltan promised himself that he would take Fido to the vet's that evening; he did not want the children noticing that Fido was under par. The illusion that Fido was a real dog had to be maintained.

Openings such as this aim to grab the reader's attention by the element of surprise, of novelty, of the unfamiliar. Very often supernatural or science fiction stories employ openings of this type.

The 'forewarning' or 'flashback' opening
Basically, these are the same types of openings except that in one the writer is forewarning the reader about something that is going to happen in the story and, in the other, past events are recalled. Here is an example:

It was to turn out to be the most important day of my life and yet I had no notion of that when the day began as usual for me.

The supplied opening
Often in exam papers candidates are given the opening sentence of a story and asked to continue it, for example:

1 I pushed open the door. The sight that greeted me was overwhelming.
2 'You'll be very sorry if you do that,' he said.

Some candidates grab at these openings as a ready-made way of getting them started in a story, but our advice is to choose this option only if you really believe you can make something worthwhile out of the supplied opening.

Exercise Write various kinds of openings for some of the following narrative subjects:

The final day   The big heat   The last goodbye   The friends   Against all the odds   The quarrel   A summer's day   Lost in the city   Just another day   The duel   The challenge   Someone is calling me

More about structure

Short stories need not be very dramatic nor filled with exciting events. Their subject can be ordinary life and small, everyday incidents. You will almost certainly write better short stories if you write about something close to your personal experience.

Try to use your own ideas as far as possible, and choose plots that can be dealt with adequately in a short story.

A 'peg' is a simple idea, perhaps an unexpected happening, a noteworthy incident, a minor theme, that can be used as the peg or hook upon which to hang a short story. The most successful short stories usually have 'pegs' of this kind; the writer has built a short story round this one central idea or incident and has concentrated on the telling of that to the exclusion of anything else. When you are thinking of a storyline for your story, try to think in terms of a simple 'peg' on which to hang it.

Endings

Endings are important in all pieces of continuous writing and equally so in stories. Just as there are a variety of openings you can use, so there are various kinds of endings.

The twist or unexpected ending

This is when you surprise the reader by ending the story in a very unexpected manner by a sudden twist of events or by letting the reader know some information (e.g. about the characters) that had been unknown to them before. To be effective, a twist ending needs to be within the bounds of credibility and be genuinely surprising. If it is too obvious, e.g. of the type where the mysterious stranger reveals himself as a CIA agent, then it will fall flat. (Remember that 'dream' endings will surprise no one!)

The 'cliff-hanger' ending

The unfinished effect can be effective, where the story builds to some climax, and then there is no definite conclusion:

> Relentlessly, as if nothing had happened, the ants continued their advance . . .

Everything is *not* neatly rounded off. The reader is left wondering what is going to happen next. Please note that this kind of ending is deliberately created and is quite different from the type of ending that is no real conclusion either because it just fades out feebly or because the writer has just run out of time.

The definite ending

At its simplest, this kind of ending is of the 'and then they lived happily ever after' variety. Obviously you will avoid using that one, but some stories can come to a neat, logical, rounded conclusion. Make sure that endings of this sort are not too short and rushed. The ending will, of course, be the last thing the examiner reads in your piece. If your story ends feebly or vaguely, then that will leave a bad impression.

Outlines

You should always create skeleton outlines for your stories. If you don't, or if you veer wildly from your original outline, you may well fall into the trap of trying to pack too many incidents into your story.

The outline should signpost clearly the various stages of the story. Included in the outline should be a definite opening and ending.

Here is a possible outline for the narrative topic 'The accusation':

> Middle-aged woman in supermarket – set ordinariness of scene – routine. Manager approaches her and asks what is in her bag; woman extremely upset and protests. Faces staring at her, somehow feels guilty; manager insists; woman refuses; manager insists on her coming to office and calls security guards; manager reveals two tins of brand cat food; woman now in tears produces receipt from another store; manager tries to bluster; profuse apologies; woman leaves shop still upset; feels humiliated.

This storyline has the merit of relating a simple incident which can be handled within the confines of a short story. It is dramatic but is set against a familiar background. It allows for some characterisation – the woman, the manager. It allows for a quiet opening with the routine scene being set in the supermarket. The ending of the woman being released but feeling humiliated is strong. The writer could introduce some other characters briefly: other customers, their remarks, and the security guards. The story has a simple 'peg' and can be handled within the length of an average story written for an examination.

Exercises

1   Write skeleton outlines for any of the following topics, making sure you create storylines that can be tackled adequately within the length of a timed essay. Pay close attention to openings and endings.

    The electronics wizard   The will to win   The misunderstanding   The journey   The letter   Broken promises

2   Write a story about a young person with a unique talent that brings mixed blessings to him or her.

3   Write a story about a young person who is the victim of snobbery, but who climbs above petty attitudes to achieve something important.

4   Write a story with this opening sentence: 'I had never felt jealousy before, but now I was very jealous indeed.'

Direct speech in story-telling

Do not overdo the use of direct speech (dialogue/conversation) in your stories. It is best to include brief snatches of direct speech, short exchanges of dialogue among the characters. Direct speech has more impact in a story if it is used sparingly.

Speech marks

The punctuation of speech is covered fully on pages 9–10, but here is a brief reminder of the need to use speech marks.

All direct speech should be enclosed within speech marks or inverted commas (' ').

> 'I'm sorry to see you here,' he said. 'Indeed, why are you here?'
> 'None of your business,' the young woman replied.
> 'Really!' he commented sarcastically.

Writing effective direct speech

The important point to note about direct speech is that it is quite difficult to write really effective dialogue. Too often, direct speech is used by candidates to fill up the page. As well as being concise, direct speech in a story should:

> inform the reader about the action or the characters;
> suit the character of the character who is supposedly speaking.

Sometimes direct speech can add an immediacy to your story-telling. It can communicate characters' anxiety, excitement, anger or amusement. If it does that effectively, then it justifies itself. If it is only a rather flat and meaningless exchange, then it does not justify itself.

Dramatising events

Direct speech can play an important part in dramatising important incidents in a story. Instead of using narrative prose, you can give the actual words of the characters:

> The teacher looked very stern.
> 'Let me see your bag, Tracy.'
> Tracy felt the red creeping into her complexion. Why did she feel so guilty?
> 'Why, Miss? I haven't done anything.'
> The teacher hesitated.
> 'Then you haven't anything to worry about, have you?'
> Tracy handed over her bag. Her heart was hammering with fear.

The use of direct speech mixed with tense narrative in that short passage helps to create a directness, a dramatic atmosphere. It is also more effective because it is concise and not over-done.

Here is another example of how direct speech can add dramatic impact. First a narrative account of an incident in a shop.

> The store detective grabbed the boy by the arm and asked him what he had in his pocket. The boy protested that he had nothing he shouldn't have in his pockets and demanded to know why he was being held. The detective said he suspected him of having stolen some sweets.

Here is the same incident but described in a mixture of narrative and direct speech:

> The store detective grabbed the boy by the arm.
> 'What do you have there in your pocket?' he demanded to know.
> 'Nothing. Just my own stuff. What are you on about? Why are you holding on to me?' the boy protested.
> 'I suspect you've just stolen some sweets,' the detective said.

The direct speech adds drama to the incident. In this case, it is more effective than straight narrative in 'capturing' the incident and holding the reader's attention.

Exercises
1   Read the following narrative extracts, then describe the same incidents using a mixture of narrative and direct speech.

(*a*)   The waitress approached the table and asked her what she wanted to order. Letty chose roast beef but the waitress said there was none left. Letty then chose lamb but again the waitress said it was off. Letty in despair then chose shepherd's pie but met with the same answer. She then asked what was available to eat and was told there were only cheese sandwiches.

(*b*)   Alan stopped a stranger in the street and asked where number 196 was. The stranger asked him suspiciously why he wanted to know. Alan said that was none of his business. The stranger said he'd make it his business. At that, Alan told him to forget it. As he walked away the stranger shouted after him that he'd remember his face.

2   Write short pieces based on one or more of the following situations; retain a balance between narrative (the prose account) and direct speech (the exchange of dialogue among the characters).

(*a*)   A teacher meets a pupil in the corridor and enquires about *either* the pupil's missing homework *or* absence from the teacher's lesson.

(*b*)   A bus conductor and a passenger have a sharp exchange about *either* the length of time the passenger has had to wait for the bus *or* the correct fare the passenger ought to be charged.

(*c*)   A heckler in a club or pub exchanges comments with a comedian on stage about the quality of the comedian's jokes.

Characterisation

You can create interesting characters in a variety of ways.

1 You can give a brief physical description which tells the reader something about the character:

> Mr Simkins usually managed to wear socks that did not match. His jackets were always wrongly buttoned so they looked as though they were ill-fitting even if they were not. His trouser legs ended six inches above the ankle. Haircuts were a rare occurrence for him and at times it seemed as though baths were as well. Altogether his appearance suggested he had been stuck together in a very haphazard way.

This description is not just description for the sake of it. It helps to convey a picture or an idea of the character; the physical details tells the reader important things about the person.

2 You can use direct speech to have your characters say things which reveal what kind of people they are:

> 'Hello, John, how's it going then? Got a new motor, 'ave you?' Ted asked.
>
> 'Yeh, got it down the auction, didn't I.'
>
> 'Most of 'em are knocked off, old son. You'll be done for receiving stolen goods.'
>
> 'Shut your north-and-south, mate. I know an 'ot car when I see one and this ain't.'
>
> 'Oh, well,' Ted said, 'suit yourself. Wouldn't touch the car auctions with a bargepole myself. Still, I expects you know what you're doing, my old china.'
>
> 'That I do,' John said confidently.

This stretch of dialogue not only communicates information to the reader (e.g. that John has bought a new car) but conveys something about the attitudes of Ted and John and the kind of relationship they have. The dialect they speak in tells us where they come from, too.

3 You can involve your characters in action sequences that reveal something of their personalities:

> The bully strode towards Janet. She wanted to run but she forced herself to stay where she was. The larger and older girl deliberately stopped in front of Janet so she could not get past. Janet moved to the side; the bully moved with her. Janet tried the other side. The bully followed suit. There was no other way out. Janet steeled herself and shoved the other girl back. The look of astonishment on the bully's face was a study!

This piece of narrative reveals Janet's fear of the bully and allows us inside Janet's thoughts: 'She wanted to run but . . .'. It then shows Janet trying to avoid trouble but deciding there was no way out: 'Janet steeled herself and shoved the other girl back.' We learn something about Janet's character from this short section.

4   You can tell the reader directly what kind of a person your character is:

> Mrs Jones was a gregarious old woman. She disliked being on her own and, therefore, she was a 'joiner' of things: clubs, societies, associations and groups. It was even rumoured that she belonged to all three main political parties merely to have meetings to go to. She would buttonhole someone wherever she went and give him or her the benefit of the wisdom of her years. Often people would find her fascinating to listen to because Mrs Jones had led an eventful life and had the gift of the gab to communicate her experiences.

Here is a short character sketch from a narrative essay that combines telling the reader directly something about the character, with physical description, and the use of direct speech to reveal personality.

> Joe was a small man and this may have accounted in part for his aggressive attitude to life. Diminutive he may have been, but his arms and legs had rippling muscles which he was fond of drawing attention to.
>
> 'You see them muscles?' he would say, bending his arm at the elbow and pointing at his biceps. 'The product of weight-training.'
>
> He would look round the company somewhat truculently as though daring someone to challenge his claim.

We learn something important about Joe from that passage. The writer tells us he has 'an aggressive attitude to life', partly because he was 'small', 'diminutive'. He illustrates the aggressiveness in the description of the 'pointing at his biceps' and uses Joe's actual words to add life to the description. We now know enough about Joe for the purposes of a narrative essay. Having built up the character economically, the writer can go on to involve Joe in his story.

Exercise   Write brief character sketches for some of the following to be used within narrative essays, employing a mixture of character description, physical description, an incident and direct speech:

> an elderly person; a person in a position of authority over young people; a sports star; a fictional detective or private eye.

Description in narrative writing

Descriptive detail can be used in story-telling to add elements of reality and vividness to the narrative and characters. Description in stories helps the reader to visualise the scenes being described; it provides a setting.

In novels, writers can often indulge themselves in elaborate descriptions. In short stories, writers have to restrict themselves to brief but effective descriptive touches. In the stories you write in an exam or for course work, you should try to include some description, but it must be appropriate and concise.

Descriptive words

Adjectives are describing words attached to nouns or pronouns.

Adverbs are words that qualify the meaning of *verbs*. Adverbs usually, but by no means always, end in -ly. They are normally next to or in close proximity to verbs.

The use of vivid adjectives and adverbs can enliven narrative writing considerably. A bare piece of narrative can become much more interesting by the addition of descriptive words. Here is a straight piece of narrative:

> She approached the house. There was a stillness to the place. She pulled the bell rope. She heard the bell ring inside. She waited for someone to come.

The style of that paragraph is rather bare and monotonous. Four of the five sentences, you will notice, begin with 'she', which adds to the monotony. However, note how the impact of the paragraph can be increased by the addition of some descriptive detail:

> Timorously she approached the mysterious house enshrouded in fog. There was an eerie stillness to the desolate place. Hesitantly, she pulled the twisted old bell rope. She heard a cracked bell ring distantly inside. Anxiously, she waited for someone to come.

Adjectives added: mysterious   eerie   desolate   twisted   old   cracked
Adverbs added: timorously   hesitantly   distantly   anxiously
Adjectival phrase: enshrouded in fog

Each of these words and phrases add to the vividness of the writing. The narrative has much more atmosphere and reality in this version. In terms of the number of words used, however, it is very economical.

Here is another example of very bare narrative:

> The singer strode onto the stage. She started to sing her latest hit. The audience went crazy. The words of the song could hardly be heard. It seemed the crowd didn't want to hear their idol but just desired to worship at her feet. She came to the end of her first number. She told them how pleased she was to be there. They cheered her words.

Below is another version of that passage with the addition of descriptive words and phrases:

> The famous singer strode arrogantly on to the brightly-lit, huge stage. Immediately she launched enthusiastically into her latest hit. The excited audience went crazy with delight. The simple words of the song could hardly be heard above the din. It certainly seemed the massive crowd didn't want to hear their idol but just desired to worship shamelessly at her feet. Suddenly she came to the end of the first number. Confidently she told the noisy audience how pleased she was to be there in that arena. They cheered her clichéd words to the skies.

> *Adjectives added*: famous   brightly-lit   huge   excited   simple
>   massive   noisy   clichéd
> *Adverbs*: arrogantly   immediately   enthusiastically   certainly
>   shamelessly   suddenly   confidently
> *Adverbial phrases*: above the din   in that arena   to the skies

Exercise Below are four passages of rather bare narrative. Rewrite all of them, adding descriptive words that enhance vividness and detail. In addition to the adjectives, adverbs, adjectival and adverbial phrases you add, try to think of more descriptive verbs than those used in the passages. The verbs are italicised in all of the passages. There are already some adjectives and adverbs in the passages; replace them with more 'vivid' words, if you like.

1 I *wanted to say* something but I *couldn't*. The tension of the occasion *was getting* to me. The faces *stared* at me. The hatred I *saw* in their eyes *frightened* me. What a fate *seemed to be* in store for me!
2 He *ran* towards the school buildings. The place *looked* very forbidding. He *darted* up the main stairs. The corridors *seemed* very long. He *dreaded* explaining to his form master why he *was* late yet again.
3 The crowd *poured* out of the ground. It *had been* a great match. Most of the spectators *would remember* it for the rest of their lives. Some supporters *were chanting* but it all *seemed* good-humoured. The police on duty at the match *did not look* concerned. The police horses *waited* for any sign of trouble. However, the excitement of the match *seemed to have used up* all the energies of the young people.
4 The house *stood* in the middle of a park. The greenery around *provided* a setting for the building. Despite this, there *was* something curious about the house, something not quite right. It *did not seem to welcome* visitors. There *was* something uninviting about it. She *approached* it. She *knocked* on the door. She *waited*. She *could hear* someone moving inside. The door *opened*.

Marked example of narrative writing
Here is a narrative piece written in response to the title 'The Letter'. It has some strengths and some weaknesses, which are reflected in the detailed marking and general comments made by the examiner.

The Letter

She heard the click of the letter box as the postman pushed the letters through. Janet stood for a while wondering whether she should go and pick up the letters herself. She knew with virtual certainty that one of them would be for her. It was a very important letter indeed and one that she had been waiting for with a mixture of dread and excited anticipation.

Sure enough, on the mat inside the door was a pile of letters and the top one was for her. In fact, the handwriting on the envelope was her own. As the school had asked all examination pupils to address an envelope to themselves ready for the dispatch of the GCSE results. Inside that letter was the key to her future, or so Janet felt at that moment.

She sat down on an armchair in the sitting room.

Self-recrimination flooded into her mind. Why hadn't she studied harder. Why had she gone out so often instead of staying at home and revising. She wouldn't be in such a panick now if she had worked harder. The echoes of advice from teachers and parents reverberated in her mind. Well, this was the day of reckoning!

Perhaps she ought to postpone the opening of the letter until she felt stronger, but that might just increase her anxiety. She felt so weak and cowardly. My goodness, it was only a letter, after all! It couldn't harm her; it wasn't poisonous. But then it was in a way. If it spelled out failure, it would spread poison throughout her life.

No, that was crazy thinking! If she had failed anything, she would simply try again. After all, she had always managed to face up to small failures before. Yes, small failures! If she had failed to gain a good grade in her English language exam, that would not be a 'small' failure. That would be catastrophic!

It would mean she wouldn't be able to take up that place at college she had been offered. It would mean she would have to mark time, as it were, for another year. The prospect of having to sitting her exams again was not an attractive one. She was eager to leave school behind her. She felt herself on the threshold of adulthood; she was anxious to move on. Failure at this point would be a

Marginal annotations:
- √ vocab.
- √ vocab.
- cont.
- grammar
- para.
- √ vocab.
- pct.
- pct.
- sp.
- √ vocab.
- vocab.
- grammar

blow to her ambitions. Life was out there waiting to be lived. She wanted to get to grips with it. She could not afford to waste any time.

Her fingers gripped the envelope tightly. She would count to ten . . . no, a hundred, then she would open it. One . . . two . . . three . . . four . . . oh, this was childish. Goodness, it was only a piece of paper. She was sixteen, wasn't she? She wanted to be adult and here she was unable to open the envelope with the results of her exams. That wasn't very adult! Perhaps she wasn't quite ready for the adult world out there.

'What are you sitting in here for?' her mother's voice said from behind her.

'Oh, nothing,' mumbled Janet.

'What's that letter you have?'

'Oh, the exam results.'

'What! Haven't you opened it?' Her mother's tone betrayed her anxiety.

'Yes, I've opened it!' Janet said, decisively ripping the envelope open.

She had passed English with flying colours! She had passed . . . no, she had only managed a low grade in Geography. The rest were a mixture of good, mediocre, and poorish grades. All in all, there were no great shocks and her splendid grade in English was a real bonus.

Oh, what a releaf! She handed the letter to her mother   sp. and went through to the dining room. She felt hungry now. Her appetite for food and for life had returned.   expression Things had worked out reasonably well – not sensationally well, but satisfactorily. The letter had not spelt out her doom. She could face the future with some confidence.

Examiner's comments:

Content: mainly follows thoughts of main character and then has mother breaking into them; works quite well; shows some insights into her feelings.

Organisation: strong opening and effective building up of tension to opening of letter. Perhaps not quite enough of the exam results themselves. Last paragraph concludes the story effectively.

Continuity and paragraphing: sustained well; one paragraph consists of one sentence only.

Accuracy: some careless spelling errors which could have been corrected during checking.

Punctuation: missing question marks.

Sentence construction: one incomplete sentence.

Vocabulary and expression: appropriate and lively expression; wide range of vocabulary.

Unmarked example of narrative writing

Here is a story written in response to the topic 'The Journey'. Read it carefully at least twice; the first time you read it, read it straight through to gain a general impression. When you re-read it, consider the following aspects: the opening to the essay; the development of the story; the relevance to the theme; the spelling, punctuation and grammar errors; the ending. Mark any errors you can find and correct them (see p. 176). Write out your 'examiner's comments' as has been done for previous marked examples.

The Journey

He was awakened in the middle of the night. Through his sleep-befuddled eyes, he could see his mother's tearful face, anxious and tired. She said something to him but he was too confused to take it in, she shook him again almost ruffly. All he knew was that he had to get up in the middle of the night for some reason.

'Get up, son. Come on, wake up. We have to catch a train,' his mother said again.

Half-an-hour later he was in a taxi headed for the station. His mother sat beside him crying into her handkerchief. He wanted to ask why she was crying but he did not want to intrude. Besides, he felt he   10
had already been told and was to embarassed to ask. It must have been something important because he had never seen his mother cry before.

The streets of the city were empty at that time of night. His mother had mumured something about catching a train at five. The only time they ever travelled on a train was when they went to his grandparents' place in the country. Perhaps they were going there now, but why at this time of night and why was his mother so upset?

They had to wait at the station for the connection that was to stop there, his mother frightened him by talking to herself as though he   20
were not sitting beside her.

'He was a good man. Always a good man. No one can speak ill of him.'

And again she cried. He suddenly realised what had happened. His grandfather had died. That was it. That was why they were making this journey.

He didn't know how he felt about this fact. His grandfather had been rather a severe man ruling over his family with a dictator's grip. He had always been frightened of him. But surely he should be feeling some sadness. His mother was obviously very upset. A stab of guilt went   30
through him.

Eventually the train came and they settled into an empty compartment. His mother gave him some attention then, as though she had suddenly realised that he was there.

'You understand what's happened, son?' she asked.

He nodded, still feeling guilty.

'It was very sudden. In his sleep. He was such a good man.'

Oh, if only he could stop her crying! If only he could cry some tears himself, but he felt no grief. The fact of his grandfather's death seemed
40   unreal to him.

Death. Died. In his sleep. The words echoed in his mind. What did they mean? He would never see his grandfather again. That was what death meant. His grandfather would not be there ruling over the old house when they got off the train at the old country station. Death meant his mother's tears. Death meant he had to get up in the middle of the night. Death was a new thing in his life.

The train swept through the suburbs of the city and into the countryside. The darkness was giving way to a gradual dawn. He had brought a comic with him to read. Could he take it out of his pocket
50   and start reading it? He covertly removed the comic from his coat pocket and started reading. If his mother noticed, she made no sign.

His favourite hero was just about to attempt to climb Mount Everest single handed and without the aid of oxygen. Last week he had won ten gold medals at the Olympics. He was not like ordinary men. No one knew how old he was. The hero was timeless. *He* would never die. He would always manage to cheat death.

Before long, he felt drowsy. The missing hours of sleep had caught up with him. When he awoke it was bright and sunny.

'We're just arriving,' his mother siad to him.
60   A few minutes later the train stopped at the familiar station. They were the only passengers to get off.

Two people were waiting for them on the platform. He recognised his aunt and uncle. They both embraced and kissed his mother. He felt left out of the grief they all seemed to share.

They walked out of the station to a waiting car. It had been an unreal journey, like no journey he had ever had before. Even now he could not really comprehend why he had come here with his mother. He knew he would remember the journey for the rest of his life, though. Some day he would understand it all.

Exercises

1 Below are further topics for narrative writing:
   The great adventure   The lucky chance   A case of mistaken identity
   Family quarrel   The final day   The injustice   A lack of responsibility
2 'Something very strange happened in the park yesterday.' Write a story
   with this opening.
3 Write a story about a person who, after many disappointments,
   achieves something he or she has been aiming at for some time.
4 'Don't mention my name. It has to be a secret.' Write a story with this
   opening.

'Oh, yes, describing things – I can do that easily!'

Too many candidates fall into the trap of thinking that if they string together 500 words of vague description, they have managed to write a good descriptive piece. However, before you take on the task of writing a descriptive piece, you must be convinced that you have enough vivid detail in your mind's eye *and* the ability to bring the detail to life in language that is imaginative and free of clichés.

Keeping to the point

One major fault to avoid is starting a descriptive piece and then turning it into a story with lots of blood-and-thunder, murder-and-mayhem and all kinds of things thrown into the plot. Consider this topic, for example:

> Write a description of a scene in the countryside on a hot summer's day.

The examiner clearly wants you to write a descriptive piece. If you start off doing so and then introduce a narrative about cops-and-robbers, then you are not giving the examiner what he or she wants.

Shaping your descriptive writing

All pieces of continuous writing should have a definite shape. There is a danger in writing a descriptive piece that you may allow the description to meander and come to no definite conclusion. You must create a structure for your description. The structure might be suggested by the topic itself; if, for example, you are given the topic 'Describe a day in the life of a busy street market', you already have a convenient structure for your essay; you can follow the day's events from dawn to dusk.

Consider this topic:

> Describe a real-life person whom you think of as being an outstanding personality.

Here you would have to find a way of introducing the person you have chosen to describe, then illustrate why you think he or she is such an outstanding personality and then draw the description to an appropriate conclusion. In other words, you will be looking for a strong opening, a structured, linked development and a definite ending to your descriptive writing.

Vocabulary and expression

To write effective descriptive pieces, you must be confident of your ability to employ a range of expression and vocabulary. Consider this extract from a piece describing a scene in the countryside on a hot summer's day:

> It was a nice, hot day. The sun was pleasant on her face as she sat on the green grass in the beautiful countryside. The birds were twittering in the trees. The gentle breeze fanned her cheeks. Somewhere over in the next field cows were mooing and sheep were baa-ing.

In this kind of clichéd description, days are always 'nice' or 'pleasant', the grass is always 'green' and the countryside 'beautiful'; birds continually 'twitter' in the trees and the breezes are always 'gentle'.

The faults in this short extract are quite obvious; the writer seems to have made little attempt to go beyond a very limited store of descriptive words and a selection of unoriginal detail. The writer has used 'second-hand' clichés and the examiner is bound to groan when he or she reads them.

However, a more thoughtful use of vocabulary applied to the same subject-matter can bring about a considerable improvement:

> The temperature was high, but not so high that it was uncomfortable. The sun warmed her face as she sat in the tranquil countryside on the lush grass. The birds were singing their mid-morning chorus in the nearby trees. The slight breeze was a welcome fan on her cheeks. Somewhere over in the neighbouring fields cows and sheep could be heard complaining that they had not been fed yet.

When you are writing a description, and this applies also to short descriptive passages you may include in narrative or personal essays, you must really try to avoid using the most obvious clichés. With a little thought it is possible to find alternatives to basic adjectives such as 'nice', 'pleasant', 'beautiful', etc., and to clichés such as birds 'twittering' in the trees.

Exercise Below are a number of short descriptive passages that are full of clichés and display a limited range of vocabulary. Rewrite each of them using a wider range of vocabulary and less clichéd expression.

1 *The tramp* The tramp wore tattered old clothes. His hair was long and his shoes were bad. His beard was untidy. He carried his poor belongings on a pack on his bent back. He was not a very nice-looking man.

2 *The park* The flower beds were very nice in the park. It was pleasant to sit in the park watching the squirrels dart about, or watch people playing games. The trees were very green and the grass grew quite long. Sometimes young people were noisy and this annoyed the older people.

3 *The weather* The sky was blue, but the weather was very cold. It was not very nice at all. The icy air froze ears and noses and the cold conditions forced everyone to wear lots of extra clothes. The unpleasant conditions meant more people stayed indoors so it was very boring.

Various types of descriptive writing

A descriptive piece may involve you in describing a place, a scene, an event or a person or persons. Within the term 'descriptive writing' there are two main categories: imaginative description and objective description. We will deal with imaginative description in this section, and with objective description in the section on directed/factual writing.

Describing a place or a scene

We have already mentioned (page 65) one topic that was about describing a place: the street market topic. By setting that topic, the examiner is giving you the chance to write about contrasting scenes in the market: when the stall-holders are setting out their stalls in the early morning, then when the crowds are busy shopping and perhaps the scene at the end of the day, for example.

Sometimes the topic itself asks you to contrast different scenes or moods at different times of the day or year, or some other contrast is asked for. If you choose to write a contrasting description of this kind, you must make sure you provide a clear contrast in your piece and that you deal adequately with both scenes.

Here are some examples of this kind of topic:

> Write a description of a railway station when it is at its busiest and then when it is virtually deserted.
> Describe a park in the centre of the city at these two times of the year – at the height of summer and in the depths of winter.
> Write a description of a funfair when there are crowds of people and when it is deserted.

If you are asked to make a contrast, as in those examples, at least you are given a ready-made structure for your writing. There will be two main sections and you will have to find a way of linking the first section of description with the second half; it would also be advisable to conclude the piece with some 'linked' material.

Here is a possible outline for the railway station topic:

1 Station in the morning rush-hour – crowds spilling out of trains – bustling hurried atmosphere.
2 Irritated people and employees – frantic rush for buses and taxis – march of the commuters.
3 Military music playing on the public address – everyone with a determined air – impersonal – anonymous in a vast army of soldier ants.
4 Contrast – late at night – the army have disappeared into their trenches ready to appear for another day's war – cleaners sweeping the railway platforms – waiting rooms with one or two sleeping occupants.

5 A few hopeful passengers scanning departure board – some drunken revellers – a few lost souls – a few furtive-looking individuals – atmosphere of a place in limbo.

6 The down-and-outs – tramp looking through the litter bins – policeman moving them on – a couple have a lovers' tiff – atmosphere of sadness and loneliness.

7 Concluding paragraph – soon the station will reverberate to military music again – crowds will reappear – the night people will have vanished – another busy day, another day of struggle.

Here is a possible outline for the 'park' topic:

1 Opening: mention stark contrast of park in summer and in winter – blooming in summer – hard struggle for survival in winter.

2 In summer: park usually crowded on fine days – families picnicking – people playing tennis/football – early morning joggers – late night lovers.

3 Flowers and trees in bloom – squirrels well-fed – birds singing – ducks in pond with young – abundance.

4 Winter shroud of gloom; trees bare – solitary figures walking – breath lingering in icy air.

5 Birds flown to distant climes – those left dependent on bread – ducks somehow survive – squirrels go into hibernation – unglamorous struggle for survival.

6 Continuity of nature – people react to seasons as plants and animals do – they struggle for existence and most desert the park until erupts into spring and flowers into summer.

When you are writing about two different aspects of a place, it is as well to use your final paragraph to make some concluding comments on the main contrasts. This draws the threads of the essay together and avoids dividing the piece into separate halves.

Avoid injecting exaggerated incidents such as a robbery or a violent scene of some kind in the mistaken notion that this will add life to the description. That is usually a sign of a writer who has run out of details to describe. Mostly, you are expected to describe a typical scene without introducing unusual events.

Exercise Write detailed outlines for one or more of the topics listed on page 66. Make sure you fill your outlines with sufficient detail to convey a vivid contrast and that you include a strong opening and a conclusion that draws the two main threads of your description together.

Describing events

Sometimes you are asked to describe an event, as in this example:

> Give an account of a special occasion of some kind in which you took part. It could have been an event connected with your family, your school or college, or some organisation of which you are a member.

You must not turn the description of the event into a story. Indeed, examiners usually mark that down as a characteristic of a weaker candidate, i.e. using *any* topic as a starting-point for a story. By all means, give brief accounts of one or two incidents that happened during the occasion, but to fill your piece with an account of a smash-and-grab robbery, or some such plot-filler, would be a major error.

Here is a possible outline for a piece on the above topic:

1 School fête – annual occasion – anxious eyes turned to weather – money raised to go towards buying mini-bus – lots of preparation by teachers, pupils and parents – turned out to be mixed weather.

2 Setting up the stalls – myself responsible for cake stall – anxious about everyone bringing cakes they'd promised – everybody turned up trumps.

3 Customers slow to turn up to begin with – crowds turned up in mid-afternoon – pleasant atmosphere – head made speech – groans – not too boring.

4 Someone relieved me at cake stall – selling well – wandered round – met lots of friends – my parents at last turned up – won prize at bingo.

5 Mishap – teacher fell into pond – 'mysterious' event – speculation – bit of excitement – everybody got soaked anyway by brief shower.

6 Clearing up – luckily all cakes sold – putting away trestle tables – grumpy schoolkeeper – handed over proceeds – head beaming with pleasure – enjoyable occasion – worthy cause and knits school community together.

To describe this kind of event effectively you need some of the skills of a reporter. You must include details of where?, who?, why?, when?, which?, how? But it is not a matter of just dry reporting. You must make the occasion 'live' for the reader by selecting interesting detail and putting something of yourself into the writing.

When you are describing an event in which you have been personally involved, the boundaries between what we have called 'personal' writing and 'descriptive' writing largely disappear. We have included describing events of this kind in this particular section to remind you of the need to select concrete and vivid detail and to use appropriate, descriptive language when describing events of personal interest to you.

The above outline includes an account of the writer's own involvement in the occasion. It gives details of the event in the first paragraph. The concluding paragraph rounds it off with the details of the clearing up afterwards and the response of people to its success.

Here is another topic, followed by a possible outline:

> Describe an occasion when a very famous person came to your area for some reason (e.g. to open a fête, or a new shop, or to make a personal appearance at a special event).

1 Famous rock singer Wee Willie Winkie – opening new youth centre – favourite of thousands of people – crowds hours before the event.
2 Excitement mounted as time neared – fans with pictures – 'We love you, Willie' badges – boisterous crowd – older people as well as young.
3 Limousine arrives – crowd surges forward – kept back by guards – Willie serenely waving and blowing kisses – noise deafening – pushing and shoving – Willie shepherded into building.
4 Unable to get seats – Willie begins his speech – over-excited youngsters – very amusing lively speech – screams of admirers.
5 Willie walks round the centre – press and TV cameras – talks to youngsters, signs autographs – makes a good impression on everyone.
6 Willie leaves to loud screams – sports centre now officially opened – great local event – occasion credit to local council – youngsters benefit from centre – long remember day Wee Willie Winkie came to town.

The above outline meets the demands of 'who?, what?, where?, when?, how?, why?' reporting. Essential information is given, but the event will be described from a personal slant. The opening paragraph will communicate essential facts about the event. The closing paragraph will round it off.

Here is a sample opening paragraph:

> The day Wee Willie Winkie came to open our youth centre! Yes, I and many others will long remember that exciting day last summer when Wee Willie officially opened the Walmslow Youth Centre. Thousands of his fans encircled the purpose-built centre hours before he was due to arrive. His fans sported large picture badges on their lapels and there were many garish T-shirts emblazoned with his name and face.

A sample closing paragraph:

> At last Wee Willie had to leave because, as he put it, he had 'an important gig at Wembley' that night. He left a youth centre officially opened. He had been the focus of attention in a very important local event, an occasion that gained the council a great deal of credit with local people. Young people in the area have already benefited hugely from the centre and they remember fondly that day when Wee Willie Winkie, the megastar of rock, the 'son of Elvis', came to town.

Exercise   Write outlines for one or more of the following topics:
1 Describe a ceremonial occasion that impressed you deeply.
2 Give a description of a family celebration that brought you pleasure.
3 Describe an important event that happened recently in your local area.

Describing people

You will probably be set topics that ask you to describe a person or persons in some way. This kind of descriptive writing usually involves you in describing personality or character, as well as physical description. Your task is to give the reader as vivid an impression of the person as you can.

Consider this topic:

> We often use the phrase 'What a character!' to describe someone we know who is interesting, unusual or eccentric in some way. Describe one or more individuals whom you think of as being interesting 'characters'.

Clearly this topic asks you to describe one or more people in some detail. Physical description, including the clothes they wear, can be included if it expresses something about them as people, but you would *concentrate* on describing aspects of their personality that make them interesting. You could describe:

> the things they say;
> eccentric little habits they may have;
> their beliefs;
> incidents they have been involved in;
> mannerisms they have.

You would have to ask yourself 'What makes this person really interesting?', and concentrate on communicating that to the reader.

Not a story!

What you must not do is start to write a description of a person and then involve the person in a story. There is a great difference between giving a brief account of one or two incidents that have involved the person you are describing, and writing a full-length story around your 'character'. Your first task is to describe, not to tell a story, in this kind of writing.

Here is a possible outline for the topic mentioned above:

1 Eccentric schoolmaster – held in some affection – adds colour and life to dull school.
2 Eccentric clothes – bow tie, odd socks, garish shirts – like the image of a mad poet.
3 In the classroom – declaims Shakespeare and poetry as though Olivier on a stage – sometimes gets carried away – but very moving at times – manages to bring literature vividly to life.
4 Amusing incident – acting out great dramatic scene – gown gets caught up in window sash/cord – hopelessly entangled – carries on regardless. Class in fits of laughter.
5 Schoolmaster who is out of the ordinary – has his faults but at least his lessons are events – other staff view him with mixture of amusement, disdain and respect – most pupils recognise his worth.

The first paragraph introduces the person to be described. It says something about what he does and why the writer holds him in such esteem. Then the second paragraph concentrates on physical description, not just for the sake of it but because the man's clothes tell us something about his personality. The third paragraph describes the teacher in action, revealing his personality through his teaching techniques. The next paragraph relates an incident that again tells the reader something of his eccentricity. The fifth paragraph shows another side of the man – his carelessness and his lack of awareness, at times. The last paragraph draws these personality traits together and sums up why the man is such an interesting character.

Sample topic and outline
Describe one or more people who have the ability to make you laugh, or to amuse and entertain you.

Here is a possible outline:

1 Two people I know make me laugh – one, Robert, brilliant mimic/ impersonator – Jan, earthy humour.
2 Robert – at school, mimics teachers/head – once caught in front of class impersonating really strict teacher – also does political/television figures.
3 Often has difficulty in being himself, sometimes a sad person – covers up with funny voices – behind surface jollity, self-doubt – may go on to take up comedy professionally.
4 Jan quite different – very much herself – down-to-earth humour, description of stuffy social occasion when her humour punctured pompous atmosphere.
5 Other occasion – job interview – got annoyed by line of questioning – started sending-up interviewer; her general tendency is to deflate – admire her wit and courage.
6 Not everyone responds to Robert and Jan's humour – some are offended, bored – cannot always bring friends together – Robert and Jan tend to compete – few people have real talent to amuse – those who can are to be treasured.

Exercise Write outlines for one or more of the following topics:
1 Describe one or more of your friends, making clear what it is you like about him/her/them.
2 Describe someone you admire for his or her values and ideals.
3 Some people have the ability to get on our nerves, to irritate us in small ways. Describe one or more people who have irritating characteristics that set your nerves on edge.
4 Some people are 'larger-than-life', it seems. They appear to have exaggerated gestures, speech or mannerisms. Describe one or more people who have this kind of 'larger-than-life' personality.

Marked example of descriptive writing
'Describe a seaside resort at two different times of the year: at the height of the holiday season and in the depths of winter.'

An out-of-season seaside resort is a very different place from the busy, crowded mecca that it becomes during the holiday season. In fact, there is a melancholic atmosphere to a resort when no visitors are flocking to the funfair or spreading themselves across the beaches. In winter there are plenty of 'Vacancies' signs in the boarding-house windows. During the summer most of the hotels and guest houses are able to display their 'No vacancies' signs.   *expression*

Not that a seaside resort at the height of the summer cannot appear melancholic at times as well! What can be more miserable than a rainy day at the seaside? Holiday-makers cannot sit on the beach so they flock into the amusement arcades, the cinemas, the indoor swimming pools, the discos or just sit in their hotels gazing at the rain as it falls. Oh, the glories of the British seaside holiday!   *cont.*

However, when the sun shines on the golden sands, when the winds have dropped to slight cooling breezes, then the seaside resort comes into their own. The ice-cream sellers make a proverbial mint; the deck chair attendants are run off their feet and the brass and military bands have huge audiences when they perform in the bandstand. Dads get down to their shirtsleeves, grans tuck up their dresses, the youngsters don their swimming costumes. The funfair is crowded and the donkeys are endlessly required to carry the really young up and down the sandy track.   *cont.*   *grammar*

The British on holiday are a phlegmatic race, at least on their own territory. It does not take much sun to appear for them to get down to the beaches. They seem to expect the British climate to dole out restricted sunny periods and temperatures that are hardly equatorial. It only needs the thermometer to reach the mid-sixties and the family are off to the beach, sitting there for all the world as though they were in the Mediterranean and the sun was blazing down.   *√ vocab.*   *√ vocab.*

People going to the seaside reseorts in out-of-season periods have no expectations of the weather, or better not have at least! When the winds blow fiercely off the sea, when the heavens open and the rain falls, when flurries of snow freeze the permanent inhabitants of

seaside towns, it is hard to beleive that these resorts are `sp.`
the scene of holiday jollity. There are no ice-cream
sellers on the front; the pier is closed up. The funfair is
locked. The deck chairs and their attendants are nowhere to be seen.

A few elderly couples walk along the promenade
where a few months before thousands of people
thronged. It is as if the resorts were in a state of hiberna- `vocab.`
tion for the winter. A few travelling salesmen take up the
rooms in the guest houses but the theatres are closed.

Gradually towards the end of April there are some
signs that life is returning to the seaside resort. The
shutters come down from the shops on the seafront. A
few visitors are seen walking briskly along the sands.
The temperatures begin to rise and winter clothes are
put away. The evenings lengthen and the first swimsuits
of the summer are spotted. The resort's tills begin to ring
again as holidaymakers spend their money. Orders of
bacon increase as the owners of boarding houses stock
up. The donkeys on the sands reappear from their winter
hibernation. The fairground reopens. The sound of
music is heard again in the air. The crowds return.

Some people seem to prefer seaside resorts during the
winter when there are no crowds and little of the vulgarity that are the features of the summer. Certainly the
ambiance is gentler, more relaxing. The slightly sad air `vocab.`
may suit some people who want to escape from the
hurly-burly of big city life. But for most people there is
little attraction in a seaside resort in winter. The frenzied
gaiety, the excitement, the crowds, the rock and the
candyfloss, the pier shows and the bands – all those
things are what most people want to experience at the
seaside in the summer and year in, year out, they are not
disappointed.

Examiner's comments:

Content and structure: opening sentence plunges straight into topic and
draws contrast between winter/summer. Rest of first paragraph provides
details of this contrast. Good detail pinpointed by writer.

Continuity: links between paragraphs consistent. Development of theme from
paragraph to paragraph. Last paragraph – effective drawing to a close and
particularly effective final sentence.

Expression: good range of vocabulary: 'melancholic', 'a proverbial mint',
'phlegmatic race', 'equatorial', 'vulgarity', 'ambiance', 'frenzied'.

Accuracy: one grammatical error: 'the seaside resort comes into their own'
should be 'into its own'.

Sentence construction: length and type of sentences varied – not just a
succession of simple short sentences.

Unmarked example of descriptive writing

Describe the two people you would choose as companions for a year on a desert island. The two you choose can be real or imaginary, living or dead, famous or people you know personally.

Below is an unmarked essay in response to this topic. Read it through at least twice. There are some errors in it – pick those out and correct them. (See p. 176 for corrections.) Consider the structure, development and expression of the essay and write examiner's notes.

The two people I would choose as desert island companions would possess complementary qualities. The limitation to two people for a whole year would force me to choose two contrasting individuals who would be able to live amicably with each other and with me. Taking everything into consideration, I would choose my friends, Elsa and Jack.

Being stuck on a desert island might not be that hilarious an experience. I would certainly find it frustrating and would look to my companions for support and amusement. Elsa would supply both in
10　abundance. She is one of the most amusing people I know. Her humour defies description in a sense, because I have often tried to communicate her wit and charm to people who don't know her, but with limited success. Her humour depends not on what she says but on the way she says it. Her whole personality, which is effervescent, shapes her humour, so when I try to imitate it, it tends to fall flat. Her companionship would be ideal because she would be able to raise our spirits with her unquestionable energy and vivasity.

I can imagine you are wondering whether such endless good humour would in time become irritating, especially if times became difficult on
20　the island and hard work were required. I agree with these doubts but would clear Elsa of the charge of being superficial and shallow. I remember when I was feeling very sad about the illness of someone very close to me, she realised I was not in the mood for jokes or humour of any kind. Nevertheless, she managed to make me feel better at this time of great anxiety by her concerned sympathy. There would be many ocasions on a desert island when I would look for consolation rather than good humour.

To balance Elsas qualities I would choose Jack. Because Jack has a relaibility of caracter and a practicle frame of mind that would be of
30　great value on a desert island. Jack's physical appearance in itself is solid enough. He works outdoors and so he is always brown and weather-beaten. His build is fairly massive without edging into fat and he exudes strength and dependability.

Imagine what life on a desert island would be like. To make life bearable we would have to construct a place to live, find ways of

growing our own food (probably) and build protection for ourselves against typhoons, tornados, hurricanes and whatever else besets the inhabitants of desert islands. Jack is the original Jack-of-all-trades. He can turn his hand to almost anything and indeed is quite proud, in the nicest possible way, of his prowess. In addition to this, he is willing to 40
make his skills available to help other people, as I have discovered often enough. Once I needed a bookcase for my room, he made one without telling me about it and presented it to me on my birthday, Jack is that kind of person.

Jack would balance my tendency to get depressed and Elsa's bubbliness. He lives on a fairly even keel, exudes patience and quiet concern. If times get rough, then he would be a person to depend on. Once when I was moving house, he helped me shift my possessions in a hired van. To my shock a new pine table I had bought would not go through the front door of my new home. Calmly Jack unscrewed the front door and 50
we managed to manipulate the table into the hall, only to find we could not get it into the dining room. Therefore, Jack told me we would take it out of the window of the living room, push the table into the garden, then get it into the dining room through the door. He accomplished this with a minimum of fuss and a little help from myself. That kind of initiative and practicality would prove invaluable on a desert island.

Doubtless there would be times on the island when the three people marooned together would not get on very well. No three people can live in a confined space for a long time without other company and avoid quarrelling at times. I am convinced, however, that with Elsa 60
and Jack as companions, there would be fewer problems than usual of that kind. Both have equable personalities that allow for easy communication. Life on a desert island would be that much more bearable with them as companions.

More descriptive topics

1 Write a description of an airport departure lounge at two different times: when it is at its busiest and in the middle of the night.
2 Write a description of a crowded disco on a Saturday night.
3 A Great Sporting Occasion.
4 The Inhabitants of the Park.
5 Write a description of a zoo – its animals and visitors.

More topics for expression or continuous writing

1 'The Unexpected Windfall.' Write a story with this title.
2 'The police in this country should carry guns to combat increasingly ruthless criminals in our society.' Discuss this statement in an essay.
3 'Snow comes to the land.' Write a descriptive essay with this title.
4 'A last embrace and then goodbye.' Write a story with this opening.
5 My Neighbourhood.

Directed Writing is a form of Expression or Continuous Writing. Sometimes it comes under the heading of 'Understanding and Expression'. The examiners expect you to produce a piece of continuous writing for a specific purpose and audience out of material that is given to you.

The given material

The given material may be in the form of articles, extracts, advertisements, statements, charts, diagrams, statistics, diary extracts, newspaper editorials, interviews or letters. In an exam, you will sometimes be given a separate reading period of fifteen minutes to read through and thoroughly absorb the material.

What is being tested?

Directed writing tests several skills. First, you are asked to judge what is relevant and to select information from the given material. You then have to reorganise the relevant information you have chosen and use it in a piece of continuous writing. The purpose of the writing is clearly described in the task and the intended audience will also be clearly defined.

What does 'audience' mean?

The word 'audience' in connection with pieces of continuous writing has already been mentioned several times. Examiners are keen to test your ability to use suitable tone and language for various purposes in writing and in speech. In written pieces, you have to match the tone and language you use to the purpose and the person or persons who are going to be your readers (or the 'audience') of these pieces of writing.

To take an obvious example, consider the difference between writing a letter to a friend and writing a letter to a potential employer, whom you do not know at all. The purpose of the letter to the friend is to pass on news and gossip; naturally the tone will be informal:

> Dear Jack,
>   How's everything? Things are really boring this end at the moment, but what's new about that? I . . .

Imagine you used the same kind of tone and language to the possible employer:

> Dear Sir,
>   Thought I'd drop you a line about this job you've advertised. I fancy working for you strongly. I . . .

The tone and language of this letter are quite unsuitable. It is inappropriate for its purpose – a letter of application – and for its audience – a potential employer whom you do not know at all. This letter needs a much more formal and impersonal tone than the letter written to the friend.

This contrast is quite an obvious one, but in the GCSE course you will be expected to show you are sensitive to, and can adopt, more subtle variations of tone and language. Examination and coursework tasks may include writing any of the following:

a piece of directed writing from a list of topics you are given;
a letter of complaint to a firm or organisation;
a letter to a newspaper;
a letter as the representative of an organisation;
a letter to a friend or relative;
an article for a magazine with a particular kind of readership based on information supplied to you;
a statement for the police or an insurance company;
an argument for a case based on relevant information and opinions presented to you;
a report based on information presented in the form of lists or statistics.

Other criteria for assessment

You will be expected to write in a logical, clear manner. Your continuous writing must be expressed in your own words as far as possible, using relevant information from the given material.

You may have to write persuasively (i.e. persuading a particular readership of your point of view on an issue using arguments and facts from given information).

You may have to convey an attitude (e.g. anger or embarrassment) in a piece of writing.

You may be asked to slant material in a certain way (e.g. writing an advertisement).

You will also be tested on your ability to:

present material in an orderly way;
use vocabulary that is not just copied from the given material;
write in complete and well-constructed sentences;
avoid a monotonous and repetitive sentence construction;
use a paragraph structure correctly;
write accurately in terms of spelling, punctuation and grammar.

'Realistic' writing tasks

As far as possible, examiners will set *realistic* writing tasks in this section of the exam or course work. In preparing your response, ask yourself these questions:

If this was something I had to do for myself in real life, how would I go about it?

Would this be a suitable way of expressing myself for this purpose and to this person or persons?

What detail would I want to include in it?

What kind of tone would I use?

What is my relationship to the person or persons I am writing to? Are they like me ('my peers') or are they in a position of authority?

If you can get 'under the skin' of writing assignments like these, if you can see them as 'real' writing tasks and not artificial exercises imposed on you by out-of-touch teachers, then you will be halfway towards performing well in this section.

In the following pages you will meet a variety of directed writing tasks. Under the heading 'Method' we suggest an approach which should enable you to deal successfully with each task. Always read the 'Method' section carefully, even though it might seem to repeat advice given already. Good habits become ingrained through repetition.

We have also supplied you with sample answers. They are not the only answers that could be given – your answers will be different. They are there as guidelines for you to check your attempts against. Do not cheat yourself by reading the sample answers before writing your own answers.

Directed writing: topics

Sometimes you are merely given a list of topics for directed writing exercises, without additional information to read and extract information from. Almost always the writing assignment you are asked to do mentions a particular audience for whom you are meant to be writing.

Here are some topics of this kind:

(a) The school or college which you attend is asking for advice from pupils or students about the design of a new common room for their use. Write a piece of not more than 250 words giving your ideas of what such a common room should contain and look like.

(b) You are moving house to another area in the same city. The people who are moving into your old house do not know the area at all. You decide to write a description of the local area, mentioning anything you think might be useful for them to know, e.g. shopping facilities, transport services, location of medical care etc. Do not write more than 250 words.

(c) You have been on a train or a bus with a friend. Your friend is accused by a ticket inspector of trying to avoid paying part or the whole of the fare due. Your friend is prosecuted, but you decide to plead her or his innocence. You write a statement for the police describing what happened in not more than 250 words.

Method

The topics above supply only the bare outline of the assignment; there is no additional information for you to digest and use in a different form.

Remember you must use the question and the details given there as a starting-point. Do not change the assignment to suit yourself.

As always, you must take careful note of the audience for whom you are writing and suit your tone and language to the purpose of the piece of writing.

You must include sufficient and relevant detail in your writing. This is *factual* writing. It should be full of concrete and exact detail. It must not be vague.

Avoid monotonous and repetitive constructions; divide your piece into paragraphs; have an effective opening and ending.

Exercise   Choose one of the topics listed on p. 81. Write your piece before reading the sample answer to (*a*) below.

Sample answer to (*a*)

The room designated as the new 5th form common room is the size of three average classrooms, which means there is sufficient room to divide the common room into separate sections. The main function of the common room should be as a meeting place and club for 5th formers, but there may be occasions when some pupils wish to work in the common room, so three or four desks should be supplied and placed behind a partitioning wall.

There should be a canteen with the facilities for making tea and coffee, but not a vending machine as these machines usually provide tasteless drinks and are also quite expensive. There must be an adequate sink so that washing up can be done. Crockery will also have to be supplied, plus tea towels and washing-up liquid.

The comfort of the seating is an important factor. Pupils should be able to relax during break and lunch, and after school if they wish. Chairs and tables, as well as being comfortable and attractive, must be plentiful (to accommodate all the fifth form) and durable enough to withstand everyday use at the hands of lively young people.

Pupils should be encouraged to submit designs for the decor of the common room separately. Whatever scheme is chosen, it must be bright, youthful and relaxing, reflecting youth culture. It must not be like most school decor. There should be a notice-board which all 5th formers can use. Music ought to be allowed at certain times and, if possible, a first-class music centre should be purchased for the exclusive use of the common room.

Letters of complaint

You may be asked to write various types of letters in directed writing papers. We will start by looking at letters of complaint.

Using an appropriate tone

Examiners will be testing your ability to use appropriate tone and language in writing letters of complaint. You may have to complain about a service that proved inadequate in some way, or about some goods that turned out to be faulty. In writing a letter of complaint to a firm or organisation, there is no point in being merely abusive and impolite. Your tone should be firm but polite. You should also give full details in your complaint and the information that will enable the recipient to locate your order and any previous correspondence with you.

Below, as an example of the kind of tone to *avoid*, is a letter of complaint to a mail order firm about a tape recorder the customer has purchased.

> To whom it may concern,
>   What a bunch of cheating liars you lot are! I bought this tape recorder from you and when I received it through the post it was already broken. I'm going to report you unless I get my money back pronto. What a cheek you have! I've never been so insulted in my whole life.
>
>   Roger

What is wrong with this letter

Lay-out   All these are missing:
    sender's address; the date; the recipient's (the firm's) address;
    a proper greeting (e.g. Dear Sir,);
    a subscription or closing (e.g. Yours faithfully);
    the sender's signature (surname) and printed name.
Information   All this is missing:
    details about the tape recorder;
    invoice number/reference number; date received;
    details about what exactly is not working.
Tone and language   quite inappropriate tone; pointless abuse.

The sort of letter of complaint Roger *should* have written to the firm is shown on page 84.

Sender's address → 17 Rodway Street,
Hailsham
XY1 23Z

Date → 17th October 198–

Manager, ← Recipient's title
Audio Services, ← Recipient's address,
149 Cross Ways, with postcode
Garden City
AL9 5OK

Dear Sir/Madam, ← Greeting

I purchased a Smith-Graham cassette tape recorder, model 302, from you recently by mail order (invoice number 639640/B). It arrived on the 13th October and when I unpacked it and tried to use the machine, I found it failed to function at all.

Not only does the recorder fail to playback pre-recorded tapes, it also does not record. In the circumstances, I am returning the recorder to you in a separate package. I do not want another recorder to be sent to me, but request that the full purchase price plus the extra cost of returning it to you be refunded to me as soon as possible. My purchase was paid for by cheque (number 63352) dated 29th September.

I would appreciate your prompt attention in this matter and I look forward to hearing from you about it and having my money back.

Yours faithfully, ← Closing or subscription

Roger Law ← Signature

Roger Law ← Printed name

Closing If you address the person to whom you are writing by his or her name ('Dear Mr Smith', 'Dear Mrs Brown'), then you should use the closing 'Yours sincerely'. The difference between using 'Yours faithfully' and using 'Yours sincerely' is an important matter and examiners will expect you to get it right.

Further points

Check these four aspects of your letter:

Correct layout (check the details!).

A suitable tone is used: the tone is firm and clear, but formally polite.

Language: the words arise from the tone, and are fairly formal.

Information: it gives the references that the firm will require to deal with the complaint and states what the purchaser wants them to do.

Topics for letters of complaint

1   You have bought a series of video games from a mail order firm, address: Vizgame, Unit 32, Railsbury Trading Estate, Railsbury. You find that the video games are of a poor quality and even that some of the tapes are broken and will not play on your videotape machine. You decide to write a letter of complaint to the manager of the firm, giving full details of your purchase, the reasons for your complaint and the action you want to be taken.

2   You and a friend consider you have been treated rudely by an employee of a supermarket, bank or sports centre. Rather than complain at the time, you decide to write a letter to the manager giving exact details of the incident from your standpoint.

Letters to newspapers 1

When you write a letter to a newspaper for publication, you are hoping it will be printed on the letters page. You should address it to the Editor of the newspaper, but remember your real audience is the readers.

The letters page of a newspaper is a kind of forum where individual members of the public can express their opinions and try to persuade other readers to their point of view, on issues ranging from the very trivial to the most serious. Therefore, the techniques to be employed in writing a letter to the Editor have much in common with those used in persuasive pieces of writing. A letter to a newspaper, however, has to be short and concisely expressed. Some of the advice on how to express your opinions in a continuous piece of writing (pages 21–26) is relevant to this type of letter-writing.

Format or layout

Your address should be written as usual in the top right-hand corner, with the date below. On the left-hand side of the letter, starting a line below the date, you should write the title of the person to whom you are writing (The Editor) and the full address of the newspaper. Then, a line or two below, begin the letter: 'Dear Sir':

(your address)
25.6.8 –

The Editor,
Langley Echo,
Mason Street,
Langley.

Dear Sir,

End the letter with 'Yours faithfully' and your signature. Always print your name below, even if you think your signature is legible.

Content

It is wise to refer in your very first sentence of the letter to your topic or the editorial, article or previously printed letter that you are replying to:

'In response to your editorial in last week's issue, I would like to . . .'
'I could not agree more with the opinions expressed by Ms Jameson in her letter from last week's issue.'
'I was shocked to read about the drug abuse in our local area as reported in Rhoda Meakins' revealing article in Thursday's issue.'

This kind of reference immediately alerts readers to the topic you are writing about and gets the letter off to a brisk start.

Always try to end your letter on an emphatic or summarising note:

'I would strongly urge local rate-payers to lobby their MP and councillors to bring about a change in this foolish policy.'
'When all these points have been taken into consideration, I am sure wiser counsels will prevail.'

Tone

The tone of letters to newspapers can vary from the very light-hearted to the very formal. Certainly, examiners will expect you to choose a tone that is appropriate to the purpose of the letter you are writing, and to its topic – a light-hearted tone would not be appropriate to a letter about an air disaster, for example.

Read this article about rent arrears:

A furious row has erupted over the huge rent arrears that have been allowed to accumulate among local council tenants.

Latest figures show that over 150 council tenants owe more than £2500 in rent. A further 250 owe between £1500 and £2500, with 703 tenants owing between £1000 and £1500.

Housing Committee chief Laura Gardner said that the council has set up a rent arrears working party to look into the position. She blamed the increasing rent arrears on the fact that so many council tenants were unemployed or earned very low wages and simply could not afford to pay the rent.

Opposition party leader Tony Marlowe, however, had an angry reaction to the new figures and Councillor Gardner's explanation. He said, 'We are dismayed that the tenants have been able to run up such debts. If a tenant owes more than £2000, no rent has been paid for two to three years.' Councillor Marlowe blamed the situation on the council and irresponsible tenants.

A motion of censure on the council's handling of the rent arrears has been tabled by the opposition party for next Thursday's council meeting. This issue has aroused strong local feeling. Tenants' associations are divided in their attitudes: some, like the Thomas Aquinas T.A., support the council's attitude whilst others, like the Charles Dickens T.A., oppose the council's lack of action.

Exercise You are to write a letter to the editor of the newspaper in which this article appeared, the *Langley Echo*. In the letter you should refer to the article and some of the information and statements it contained. You should make your own opinion quite clear about the issue of rent arrears and the various views expressed about it in the article.

Letters to newspapers 2
Read this newspaper article on animal experiments.

Raid on animal laboratory

Over the weekend animal liberationists raided a local research laboratory where animals are used in tests to find out the effects of drugs. The break-in occurred at Symons Pharmaceutical Research Laboratory in Maversham Place. The raid was discovered only on Monday morning. The police were called to investigate.

'There was considerable damage to expensive equipment,' said a spokesman for the laboratory, 'and the intruders vandalised several rooms in the building. They also stole some of the animals used for research purposes.'

The *Post* has interviewed a local animal liberationist activist who claims to know the identity of the raiders. 'The public would be quite appalled at the cruelty of the practices carried out in the labs, if they knew the full story. We intend to get the facts to the public.' When asked about the illegality of the break-in and the subsequent damage to expensive equipment and buildings, the spokesman said: 'We've tried reasoning with these people but they're only interested in their profits. Direct action of this kind is the only thing they understand. There will be more incidents of this kind until these horrific experiments on defenceless animals cease.'

A spokesman for the police said they were interviewing local animal rights' campaigners and were confident they would be preferring serious charges soon. The spokesman for the Symons Laboratory insisted that such criminal actions would not effect any change in the laboratory policy.

Exercise   Write a letter to the Editor of the *Post* in response to this article. In your letter, the body of which should not be more than 200 words, you should refer to the article and make clear your own attitude to the issues raised by it.

Method
1   Read the article through twice.
2   Take down brief notes on the points you want to raise in your own letter.
3   Prepare an outline of your letter, dividing it into paragraphs.
4   Make sure you set out the letter properly.
5   Write your letter, then check it for accuracy.
6   Check it with the sample answer that follows.

11, Ladybird Avenue,
Rimmel.
26th September, 198–

The Editor,
The Post,
56 Adelaide Street,
Rimmel XY4 6AW

Dear Sir,

Although I do not condone the break-in and damage done to the Symons Laboratory (as reported in last Thursday's issue) I can understand why campaigners for animal rights take this extreme action. The blinkered attitudes displayed by the spokesman for the Laboratory in his remarks to your reporter partly explain why these activists feel there is no chance for a reasonable dialogue with research firms and why they resort to extreme actions.

There is no doubt at all that mankind inflicts unnecessary pain on animals. The argument that these scientific experiments are necessary for the advance of medical knowledge is not convincing. Human beings simply haven't the right to protect themselves from disease by deliberately inflicting suffering on dumb animals. I have seen pictures of animals in research laboratories and what these say about man's inhumanity to animals is shocking. Legislation needs to be passed urgently to protect animals against such obscene exploitation.

My attitude to the animal rights' activists is that they must find a way to put a case over to the public without recourse to such violent tactics. They should be able to harness public opinion behind their cause by peaceful means. This would achieve far more than a few criminal acts that get bad publicity for the cause they are supporting.

Yours faithfully,

James Wilson

James Wilson

Examiner's comments:
Lay-out: Sender's name and address correctly placed, but postcode missing. Date below. Recipient's title and address correctly placed, with postcode attached.
Correct closing or subscription.
Content: Three paragraphs: an introductory paragraph making reference to the article and making clear the writer's attitude to the issue. 2nd paragraph: development of reasons for holding this opinion. 3rd paragraph: returns to subject of animal rights' activists and expresses closing opinion.
Tone and language: fairly formal and serious tone as is suitable for letter to newspaper on an issue like this. Avoids over-stating case.
Accuracy: no spelling or grammar errors.

Letter on behalf of an organisation

You may be asked to imagine that you are the representative of a club or group and write on its behalf to a council or organisation. For example, the local council in your area puts the following advertisement in the local newspaper.

Can we help you to help yourself and others?

Are you a member of a voluntary group trying to meet some essential need in the local community? Are you thinking of setting up such a group?

Your local council is here to help you. Perhaps with advice and the skilled help of our professionals. Perhaps even with grants of money.

The council is keen to encourage local people to take the initiative in improving the quality of life for all kinds of people. This initiative could be in the field of helping people with special problems of health or loneliness. It could be a project to help make life more interesting for young people. You could be involved in the arts (music, drama, film, video, dance) or in sport. You might want to start a tenants' or residents' association.

Whatever you want to do, we want to hear from you. We guarantee your ideas will be listened to sympathetically. If you have an idea that is practical and likely to be beneficial to the community, then we will help you as much as we can. Perhaps with financial aid. Perhaps with premises. We can help in several ways.

So why not write us giving full details of the kind of project you are presently involved with or that you would like to start in the future with our help. Please give as many details as possible in your letter. The person to write to is:

> June Ashley
> Community Groups Section
> Town Hall, Glenn Street, Fordton

Exercise Write a letter to the employee of the council named in the advertisement. State the project, group or organisation you are involved with or hope to start. Make clear what its aims are and what help you think the council could give you. The body of your letter should consist of no more than 250 words.

Method

1 Read the advertisement carefully. There are several suggestions in it about the kind of activity the council would be interested in helping you with.
2 Decide on the activity or project you want to write about in your letter.
3 Add some notes about it.
4 Prepare an outline of your letter.
5 Write the letter, making sure that the lay-out is correct.
6 Check your letter with the sample answer that follows.

176, Danby Avenue,
Fordton.
14th July, 198–

June Ashley,
Community Groups Section,
Town Hall, Glenn Street,
Fordton.

Dear Ms Ashley,

A few of my friends and I are involved in a music-making project in the local area which aims to encourage people, especially the young, to play music which reflects their ethnic backgrounds and which may be performed in front of local audiences. We usually meet at the Stewart Road Community Hall on Tuesday and Thursday evenings.

We are a voluntary organisation and we are currently not funded by any outside body. Members make a weekly contribution and the Community Hall gives us free use of its premises. We desperately need financial aid to purchase new instruments, to fund local tours for performance purposes and to pay the growing costs of administering the group. Advice from experienced professionals about how to organise these activities and attract more people to take part would also be invaluable. We would like to discuss with you the possibility of the Council's funding of a full-time worker to run the project.

At present we have a membership of forty, including people of all ages between 14 and 45. We think the project provides excellent opportunities for people to learn to play instruments and perform their music in public. I hope you can help us with advice and finance.

Yours sincerely,

Sandra Atkins

Sandra Atkins

Examiner's comments:
Lay-out: sender's address and the date correctly placed. Recipient's name and address correctly placed and accurately copied from advertisement. Has chosen to use the greeting 'Dear Ms Ashley', which is appropriate because of the friendly wording of the advertisement. ('Ms' is now an accepted alternative to 'Miss' or 'Mrs'.) 'Yours sincerely', ends the letter because the recipient's name has been used in the greeting: 'Dear Ms Ashley, . . .'. The writer's name is printed below her signature to make sure it is legible.
Content: letter is well constructed. The first paragraph makes clear the point of the letter. The second paragraph develops this theme, explaining why the group needs help. The fourth paragraph effectively closes the letter.
Tone and language: the style is entirely appropriate for the purpose of the letter and the 'audience' – a council employee. It is concisely written.
Accuracy: no spelling or grammar or punctuation mistakes.
Summary: a well-written letter that would bring forth a favourable response.

Letter to a friend

Below are extracts from a holiday brochure about Eilat in Israel. Read them carefully and try to separate in your mind the general attractions of Eilat as a holiday centre from the details, and exaggerations, supplied in the brochure extracts. Then write a letter to a friend giving your reasons why you think you and she/he should choose Eilat for your next holiday venue. In the letter, you should also make a recommendation about the timing of the holiday and the hotel you should book, after having taken into account the information supplied. Your letter should consist of no more than 200 words.

Israel is a very small country, only about the size of Wales, yet mile for mile it has more places of historical and religious significance than almost anywhere on earth. However, you shouldn't get the idea that all Israel has to offer are the sunbleached remnants of an absorbing past. This country may be a museum, but it's the friendliest and liveliest and most picturesque museum in the world.

Your resort

Eilat stands at the southernmost point of Israel wedged between the brilliant blue waters of the Red Sea and the desert wilderness of the Negev with its jagged mountains, weird rocks and weatherworn canyons coloured in every shade of red, purple and yellow – the views at dawn and sunset are unforgettable.

Not so long ago Eilat was only a tiny town, a far cry from the time when it was the base for Solomon's ships bringing gold from Ophir and the harbour where he met the Queen of Sheba. Nowadays, it's a booming port once again as well as a lively resort with gleaming modern hotels lining its fine sandy beaches and with a good choice of shops where you can browse for souvenirs like exotic sea shells and malachite jewellery.

You couldn't wish for a better winter climate. The sun is strong, the desert air pleasantly dry and rain a welcome rarity – there are only half-a-dozen or so rainy days the whole year!

Sports

Not surprisingly, Eilat is a mecca for watersport enthusiasts. With water temperatures hardly ever dropping below 70 degrees fahrenheit this is the perfect place to fall off a sailboard or water-skis, and the crystal-clear waters are a paradise for snorkellers and scuba divers. If you want to stay dry, but still enjoy the kaleidoscope shoals of fish teeming amidst the coral, you can ride in a glass-bottomed boat, or visit Eilat's famous underwater observatory.

Nightlife

Eilat also has a good choice of discos and nightclubs as well as several Kosher and international restaurants serving everything from pizzas and burgers to seafood and oriental dishes.

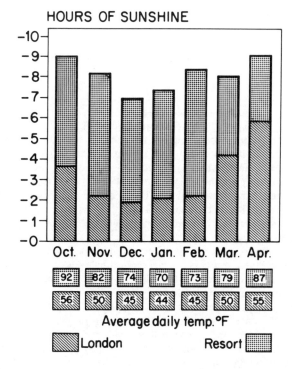

HOURS OF SUNSHINE

Average daily temp. °F

London   Resort

Method

1 Read the material through carefully at least once.
2 Check again what the examiner has asked you to do.
3 Read the material again, this time taking brief notes on information you will need for the letter.
4 Make a brief paragraph plan of the letter.
5 Write the letter.
6 Check it for accuracy and make sure you have included all details you have be asked for.

The setting out of letters Different types of letters require different formats, or different ways of laying out the content. For this assignment, we have used a particular format which is appropriate for a letter to a friend. If you want to check the format, including the position of the address, the date, the greeting and subscription (or complimentary close), you can do so on pages 81–2. However, do not compare the content of that marked example with your letter until you have completed the assignment.

Marked example of letter to a friend

Your address →   17 Abercrombie Avenue,
                        Dalgarth.

Date →   19th March

Dear Jane,   ← Greeting
        I think I've found the perfect venue for our winter holiday –
Eilat in Israel. It has most of the features we want: sun, sandy beaches and
many fascinating places of historical interest, exotic foods and first-class
accommodation. For example, in January the average daily temperature in
Eilat is 70 while we are shivering in the low 40s, or lower! Eilat rests beside
the warm Red Sea and has obviously been developed as a modern holiday
resort. However, it is in the heart of a land that has tremendous historical
and biblical significance. It seems to bring together the very ancient and the
very modern.

Eilat is on the edge of the Negev Desert and yet we will be able to indulge
in all kinds of water sports in the lagoon or the Red Sea itself. Bethlehem
and Jerusalem are within easy travelling distance. We would never be in
danger of not having things to do.

I suggest we try to book for 14 nights in the Hotel Edomit between the 8th
and 23rd of January. This will cost £301 each plus £11·55 flight supplement
and insurance, but I am sure we will get value for money. Think of those
wonderful Israeli fruits, salads and fish, and contrast shivering in a British
January with basking on an Eilat beach! I enclose a copy of the ad. so you
can judge for yourself.

Please let me know what you think as soon as possible.

Regards,   ← Subscription

                                ← Your signature

Examiner's comments:
Format: appropriate for letter to friend.
Content: essential information included; general points made. Has used
     information from brochure well, e.g. temperature, sports available, hotel
     prices.
Tone and language: personal and friendly, but also concise and business-like,
     as suits subject of letter.
Accuracy: no errors.

Articles: example 1

Below are a number of suggested 'rules' for air travel. Imagine you have to write an article for a school, college or 'in-house' magazine which will give advice about how to prepare for air travel in particular, and contain some general travel hints as well. You decide to use the information/advice below as a starting-point for your own article, but, as far as possible, you will write the article in your own words and give only what you consider to be the most essential advice. You should not use headings or number the 'rules' as has been done in the article below. You are asked to write a piece of continuous prose in not more than 200 words.

Rules of Travel

1 Find the passports now. The night before a 6am check-in is no time to be rummaging. If you've applied for new ones which haven't arrived and time's getting short, ring up the Passport Office (early in the morning).

2 Check insurance. Make sure you're covered by a big enough umbrella – particularly if you plan to practise active sports.

3 Luggage – wheel it away. Don't waste money on a case with protruding rollers – the recessed type survives carousels much better. Go for bright colours for instant visibility or band with a lurid strap.

4 Money. The most convenient way is still traveller's cheques (remember *dollar* cheques for USA and keep all numbers separate from the cheques) and a small amount of local currency. Banks also issue Eurocheque encashment cards (two cheques a day up to £50 each, written in sterling). It may be worth using the hotel change facilities and losing the odd penny for sake of convenience. Remember – restaurants which take credit cards are usually the more expensive ones.

5 Packing. As James Cameron, one of the world's great foreign correspondents, once said, 'Take twice the money and half the clothes'. Most Mediterranean holiday resorts are super-casual. Only in the Third World is a suit necessary – Indians, in particular, expect and approve of formality. In general, feet dictate. Serious sight-seeing needs sensible shoes.

6 Hand baggage. This is the survival kit. It should hold all travel documents, valuables, prescriptions, spare contact lenses or spectacles, pills and/or Pills, washing things and a swimsuit. Most important of all – passports, tickets and travellers' cheques.

7 Confirm all travel details. Which airport? Which terminal? Dates and check-in times? Name of airline handling your flight? And, before setting off (in plenty of time) telephone to check that there are no delays.

8 Dress comfortably. To keep packing light, try and wear clothes that will be useful on holiday. Neutrals travel well. And wise women wear separates – if cases get delayed or lost, it's easier to cope.

9 Complain with conviction. And follow through. If cases don't turn up on the carousel, check any others lying around. Then report the loss immediately. Fill in the Property Irregularity Form, describing in detail the case and contents. Add the baggage tag number but DO NOT give up the original tag. Report loss to the rep. and ask for emergency cash to buy essentials. Keep all receipts for insurance.

Get the rep. on your side. If the hotel's been switched, the rep. may let slip when the switch was made (useful for official complaints). Usually tour companies move you to a better hotel – at no extra cost. Watch that – in a more expensive hotel, the extras cost extra.

Write a short formal letter there and then. Give that to your rep. and get a signed receipt. As soon as you get home, write to the Customer Service Manager. Date the letter (preferably typed) and keep a copy. If this doesn't get results, move on to the Managing Director.

10 Beware of car hire. Whenever you rent, check brakes, clutch, lights *before* driving off. If there's a bargain at El Balmoral Luxury Autos, get out the fine tooth comb.

11 Take care of yourself. The danger of flights, accentuated by alcohol, is dehydration. Take plenty of water with it. Once in the sun, keep up the liquid level with mineral water and use it to clean teeth too. If you're in a dodgy area, avoid ice, uncooked food, and unpeeled fruit.

Method
1 Read the original material through once.
2 Now read it again carefully, this time taking brief notes.
3 Check it through again to make sure you haven't missed out anything essential.
4 Use your notes to make a brief structured outline for your article.
5 Now write the article, checking it over when you have finished and ensuring that you have not used more than 200 words.
6 When you have satisfied yourself that you have done the best you can, compare your attempt with the marked example below.

Marked example of answer to *Articles: example 1*

You should have checked your passports well before your flight day and also made sure you have adequate insurance cover. Luggage with wheels is recommended, but never pack any valuables in cases. The most convenient way to carry money is in the form of traveller's cheques. As casual clothes are acceptable in almost every country, it is a mistake to take too many clothes with you, but do take some sensible walking shoes. You must keep all your valuables and travel documents in your hand luggage, as well as useful first-aid items and spare spectacles, etc.

Always make sure you know all the vital details of your travel arrangements. Wear light, comfortable clothes for the flight, the kind that will be useful on holiday.

If your luggage is mislaid on the journey, fill in the relevant form there and then and inform the holiday rep. On arriving back home, write to the Customer Manager about your grievance, retaining a copy of your letter.

If you hire a car on holiday, check its condition very carefully. Be extra careful about local drinking water, especially in 'dubious' countries.

Examiner's comments:
Content: within 200-word limit; includes all essential details.
Style: concise, business-like; manages to be clear and informative.
Accuracy: no spelling or grammar errors.

Articles: example 2
Read the following extracts from an advertisement issued by the Advertising Standards Authority. Then use any relevant information from the extracts as evidence in an article you are to write for a newspaper in which you are arguing the case for one or the other of these points of view:

Advertisements in this country are under adequate control, especially with ASA supervision.

The advertising industry needs more rigorous controls than at present exist.

Your article should take one or other of these standpoints. Whichever point of view you argue for, you must use material from the extracts as relevant to your argument. Your article should consist of no more than 200 words.

DO SOME ADVERTISERS GIVE YOU TOO MANY FACTS AND TOO LITTLE INFORMATION?

It is not difficult to find yourself blinded by science.

Some advertisers are so wrapped up in their own jargon they fail to realise that to most people it's nothing more than mumbo jumbo.

But how can you be sure the facts and figures you read are accurate? And how can you tell if an over-abundance of them is not just a whitewash to conceal the truth?

SORTING OUT THE WHEAT FROM THE CHAFF.

The answers lie in a book of rules called The British Code of Advertising Practice.

It is our job as The Advertising Standards Authority to administer these rules.

WHEN ONE AND ONE MAKES SIX.

In protecting the public from being misled we are often accused of being pernickety.

We once received a complaint that a car with a 1442cc engine had been advertised as a '1·5'.

People 'in the know' apparently accept this as normal. But our complainant pointed out that his employer's mileage allowance for a '1·5' was for engines over 1451cc.

READING BETWEEN THE LINES.

It's not enough for a building society to promise 'worth 13·93% to basic rate income tax payers' when the actual interest rate can fluctuate. This must be made clear.

A hi-fi manufacturer should not merely advertise that his equipment develops a certain number of watts.

Since there are several different ways of measuring sound output, he should state which method he used and give the reader a fair basis for comparison.

And as for computers it is not on to advertise what a piece of equipment will do and simply assume that the reader will know he needs several other items in order to operate it.

So we encourage the public to help by telling us about inaccuracies we may not have spotted. Last year over 7,500 people wrote to us.

Every complaint is considered and if necessary submitted to our experts before we make a ruling.

CAN ADVERTISERS RUN RINGS ROUND US?

The ASA was not created by law and has no legal powers.

Not unnaturally some people are sceptical about its effectiveness.

In fact the ASA was set up by the advertising business to make sure the system of self-control genuinely worked in the public interest.

For this to be credible the ASA has to be totally independent of the business.

Neither the chairman nor the majority of his council members is allowed to have any involvement in advertising.

Though administrative costs are met by a levy on the business, no advertiser has any influence over ASA decisions.

Advertisers as a whole accept it is as much in their interests as the public's to keep on the right side of the rules.

The Advertising Standards Authority
If an advertisement is wrong, we're here to put it right.

Method
1   Read the material through once.
2   Make up your mind *which* point of view you are going to adopt.
3   Read through the material again, taking notes about points you think are relevant to the case you are going to make, including some points for arguments for the opposing point of view.
4   Then prepare a brief outline of the article.
5   Write the article, making sure you do not use more than 200 words, and then check it for accuracy.
6   When you have finished, compare your attempt with the marked example below.

Marked example of answer to *Articles: example 2*

I would argue that the advertising industry is under sufficient control through the Advertising Standards Authority. Rules governing advertisements are clearly laid down in 'The British Code of Advertising Practice'. The ASA considers it its role to see that these rules are observed.

The examples quoted in the advertisement give convincing proof that the ASA knows how to defend the public interest. For example, the fact that building societies in their adverts have to make clear the actual rate of interest investors will receive and that computer manufacturers must state what accessories are required to operate their machines can be put down to the ASA's attention to the detailed wording of advertisements.

The ASA welcomes complaints from the public and every complaint is given serious consideration. Although the ASA has no legal powers and was set up by the advertising industry itself, it is independent of the business; the majority of the council members have no connection with advertising. The existence of the ASA is evidence that the advertising industry wants to control itself. Despite the arguments of sceptics who say the ASA is not a powerful body, I would say advertising is properly controlled.

Examiner's comments:
Style: appropriate to the purpose and audience; clear, concise and firmly persuasive. Avoids gross exaggeration.
Content: uses points from the original advertisement to back up argument.
Organisation: clear opening and closing sentences. Developed argument in body of essay.
Accuracy: no errors.
Sentence construction: sound and varied sentences.

Articles – example 3

Below are extracts from a leaflet issued by one of the major banks about Budget Accounts. You have been asked to write an article for a booklet which gives advice about financial matters to school-leavers. Your topic is Budget Accounts. You should explain briefly what a Budget Account is, how it operates, what it costs to run and any disadvantages or advantages it may have for young people.

Who Wants a Budget Account?

You have got to pay those household bills such as gas, electricity and telephone. You find them arriving all at once before pay day. Don't worry. Just relax and send off the money.

A Budget Account eases the strain.

Running the Account

It is all so easy. Take a look at last year's bills if you can find the counterfoils tucked away, or make an estimate. Add on around 10% for the inevitable price increases. Fill in the schedule opposite and don't forget to allow a bit extra for those unexpected items. Divide the total by 12 and that is the amount you will need to transfer from your Current Account to the Budget Account every month. We can arrange the transfers so you don't have to remember every time.

You can pay the bills you've budgeted for as they arrive knowing that over the 12 months your monthly transfers and your bills will balance.

Paying the Bills

We give you your own Budget Account cheque book so you can pay the bills whenever you want. Or, if you prefer it, you can let us pay them by direct debit or standing order and debit your account. We will send you a statement every three months to help you keep track of your money.

Opening a Budget Account

Applying for a Midland Budget Account could not be easier. Complete both the schedule and agreement form and send to your branch. We will return one of the schedules to you when the account is opened so that you've got a permanent record of your calculations. If you want to include any existing direct debits or standing orders, that's O.K. by us. Just let your branch know.

If there is anything else you would like to know about Midland's Budget Account, call at any of our branches. You will find our staff ready to help you.

Interest rates and charges

Interest will be charged at 20% per annum **(APR 21.5%)**.

Rates will vary from time to time in line with the general level of interest rates and any changes will be announced in branches and in selected newspapers.

There is an annual charge of £10. Cheques, standing orders and direct debits will be charged at the bank's published personal Current Account tariff. All interest and charges will be debited to your Current Account every three months.

The Budget Account is only available to residents of the British Isles. Midland Bank credit facilities are normally available only to persons of 18 years of age or over.

Method
1 Read through the material carefully.
2 Read it again, this time taking brief notes on relevant, essential points.
3 Prepare an outline of the article you are going to write.
4 Write the article, then check you have included all essential information, and checking also for accuracy.
5 Compare your article with the sample answer below.

Marked example of answer to *Articles: example 3*

Are you facing up to paying huge bills for repairs to your motor cycle or for your holiday? Are there certain times in the year when you feel overwhelmed by the amount of money you have to pay out? If so, a Budget Account may be the answer to your worries.

A Budget Account enables you to avoid being faced with mountainous bills you cannot afford to pay, by spreading them evenly across the year. To have a Budget Account, of course, you first have to have a Currant Account in operation. With a Budget Account you work out how much money you will need to pay all your bills over a period of a year, then divide that amount by twelve. Each month the bank will transfer that amount from your current account to your Budget Account.

The bank will give you a Budget Account cheque book to pay for all the bills you have put on your list. Even when large bills come in you can still pay for them, even though the amounts may be much larger than the monthly amount you transfer to your Budget Account. Always remember that you pay interest on the extra amount that you borrow from the bank. This is not a free service! In addition there is an annual charge of £10, so even if your monthly bills exactly equalled the amount you transferred from your Currant to your Budget Account, you would still be paying the bank something for the fasility.

Therefore, a Budget Account may be very useful for young people because it is often very difficult to meet heavy bills. A Budget Account may take care of a lot of worries. However, if your bills mount up and you find yourself paying a lot of interest to the bank, then it can be a very expensive way of getting rid of one worry and replacing it with another – how to pay for the interest charges!

Examiner's comments:
Format: no guidance on length is given but this acceptable. Not too short and not too long. Written in paragraphs which are linked.
Content: explains what Budget Account is, how it operates and gives advice. However, could have mentioned that Budget Accounts are available only to persons 18 and over. Has a strong opening and an effective ending.
Tone and language: appropriate to the audience – young people.
Accuracy: two careless spelling errors: facility, current.

Making a statement as a witness

Below is a diagram of an accident involving a van, a car and a cyclist, which took place at 4.10pm on 27 March in Hailsham High Street.

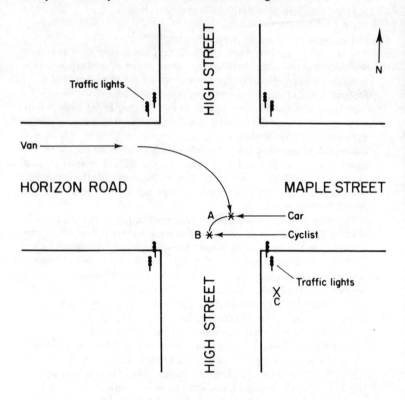

A – point of collision between van and car
B – point of collision between car and cyclist
C – position of witness

Imagine you are the witness whose position in the diagram is indicated by a cross and the letter C. You have to write a statement for the police describing in exact detail the accident as you saw it. You have to give a clear, precise description of the incident, mentioning street names and any other relevant facts, e.g. the directions the various vehicles (the car, the van and the bicycle) were travelling in, changing of traffic lights, etc. You can give an opinion about whose responsibility the accident was. Your statement should not be longer than 200 words.

Method
1 Study the diagram very carefully and work out how the collisions happened.
2 Try to see the incident from the standpoint of the witness. What would he or she have seen?
3 Write down brief notes that you think are important for the statement.
4 Prepare a brief outline of the statement.
5 Write the statement, then check it with the sample answer below.

Sample answer to *Making a statement*

I was returning home from school along the High Street, on the right hand side going north, at 4.10 p.m. on 27 March. I was approaching the traffic lights at the junction of Maple Street and the High Street, when I witnessed an accident involving a van, a car and a cyclist. The van swerved into the car and the impact of that collision forced the car to collide with the cyclist who was knocked over and received serious injuries.

I saw the whole incident clearly because my attention had initially been drawn by the car's unusual colour. The car may have been rather slow in moving away from the traffic lights when they changed to green. The van was signalling to turn right and appeared not to wait for the car to pass before doing so. The collision between the van and the car occurred, and the car, which appeared to swerve to the left, in turn collided with the cyclist. In my opinion, the cyclist was entirely blameless because he was merely proceeding across the junction.

From my standpoint it seemed that the van had arrived at the lights at Horizon Road at a fair speed, anticipating the change to green. The driver seemed to think he could turn right without waiting for the slow-moving car to pass. Although he braked suddenly, he could not pull up sufficiently quickly to avoid the collision.

Examiner's comments:
Format: divided into three paragraphs, each paragraph having a reason for its separate existence.
Content: detailed and avoids unnecessary repetition. Expresses opinion about responsibility in sober way.
Accuracy: no errors.

You might be presented with a series of statements, plus, perhaps, some material in the form of statistics or graphs, and asked to argue a case for or against an issue, referring to the statements or the opinions expressed in them and to the information contained in any additional material. You will be encouraged to add your own points to the arguments about the issue, but you will also be expected to use the given material and to incorporate it in a piece of continuous writing.

Arguing: example 1
'Equality'
Study the comments below about equality and then write a piece of no more than 300 words putting your own point of view about the issues raised. By adding points of your own, develop your argument about what equality means to you and how far you think people today are really equal.

'Equality is just a pipe-dream. People are not equal and never will be, because they are born with different talents and different wills. Those who argue for equality want everyone to be on the same mediocre level.' (Member of Parliament)

'Equality of opportunity is what we must all be arguing for and nowhere is it more important than in the field of education. At present too many of our young people do not get a fair crack of the whip.' (Teacher)

'Men do not want women to be equal. It threatens their position in society so women will have to fight every step of the way to become equal citizens.' (Journalist)

'Racial discrimination is the most important factor in creating inequality in our society. Until blacks and whites are completely equal, then there will be huge injustices practised every day we live.' (6th former)

'I don't want to be equal. I want to be myself, an individual, free of the pressure to be like everybody else. Equality means conformity as far as I'm concerned and I don't want anything to do with it.' (Student)

Method
1 You do not need to use all of the statements in writing your piece; you may pick out the statements that mean most to you and develop the points that you want to make about them.
2 Read through the statements at least twice.
3 Make brief notes about the points they raise for you.
4 Prepare an outline of the piece you want to write.
5 Write the piece, then check it for inaccuracies.
6 Check your attempt against the sample answer that follows.

Sample answer to *Arguing: example 1*

I disagree strongly with the MP's assertion that equality is a pipe-dream. People do have different innate abilities but that is not an argument which justifies inequality. The teacher's emphasis on equality of opportunity is much more in line with my thinking. There are obvious inequalities in our education system; evidence shows that how well you perform in that system largely depends on your social class, sex and race.

Sexual and racial discrimination are two extremely important factors in prolonging inequality in our society. The journalist is quite correct in stating that women will have to fight to achieve equality with men. Similarly, the sixth former's statement that colour prejudice creates huge injustices in our society is very true. To get rid of sexual and racial discrimination from society is very important in helping to create a more equal society.

The religious point of view, as expressed by the evangelist, may well be true for those who believe that the solution to society's problems lies in another world but, in my opinion, it is not much consolation to those who are suffering from the effects of terrible inequality in the here-and-now. The 'I'm an individual' argument of the student is a limited one, because no one lives in isolation from society. We are all individuals, but are also part of the society we live in. We are all affected by its laws and injustices. Burying our heads in the sand and ignoring inequalities is no solution. Therefore, I believe in a society that aims to make equality of opportunity and equality under the law a reality. Currently, many people are suffering because there is no real equality in our society.

Equality does not mean that everybody has to be the same. Equality means everybody has the right to develop in his or her own way. Considering the many different personalities people have and the marvellous opportunities a free society offers, it seems very unlikely that people in a truly equal society would develop in the same way. Variety would be the result of equality of opportunity.

Examiner's comments:

Format: four paragraphs showing some logical development. Has a definite ending.

Content: uses all the comments, but only to develop them with points to back up own point of view. Effective opening making clear own attitude.

Tone and language: concise style with appropriate tone and language. Firmly makes a case for own point of view but avoids sweeping condemnations of other views.

Accuracy: no errors.

Arguing: example 2
'Smoking'

Read the following information about smoking and then argue the case for smokers giving up the habit. You should try to answer the case made in (*a*) by Mabel Tomkins and refer also to information in (*b*) and (*c*). Do not merely copy figures, however. You may include any other relevant information or experience of your own.

(*a*) 'Smoking is such a habit with me that I know I wouldn't be able to give it up. I need cigarettes to keep me going. I smoke on social occasions and when I'm on my own. I tried giving it up once but I got so nervous and put on so much weight through eating sweets that I started to smoke again. As for lung cancer, I think to myself that it'll never happen to me.' (Mabel Tomkins)

(*b*) How to overcome the craving

'If smokers are not strongly motivated to stop, then no treatment will work whereas if they are then most treatments will work . . .' So says Martin Raw, Department of Psychology, St George's Hospital Medical School, London.

It is nicotine that seems to keep people smoking, but it is not clear how important nicotine is for lighter 'social' smokers. Few smokers are entirely nicotine addicts or pure social smokers, says Raw.

Treatment clinics, of which there are around 50 in England and Wales mostly funded by area health education departments, can help with treatments but mainly offer group discussion, mutual support and health information. Long-term success rates of between 10 and 20 per cent can be achieved, it is claimed.

Drug therapy to help kick the habit has included tranquillizers to relieve withdrawal symptoms, but Raw says there is no evidence they are effective.

Various substitutes for tobacco constituents like nicotine have emerged from time to time, but have not proved particularly effective. There are products which claim to alter the taste of cigarettes. Raw rates these as mostly quite harmless and might help smokers already determined to give up.

But the recent development of nicotine chewing gum he rates as extremely promising. It was developed by a Swedish company AB-Leo of Helsingborg. It is sold under the brand name of Nicorette and it costs about £7 for two weeks' supply. Late last year a medical tribunal ruled that the National Health Service should be prepared to pay, the product being available only on prescription.

(*c*) Britain's hidden holocaust

There are about 16 million cigarette smokers in Britain and around another two million who smoke either cigars or pipe tobacco. Non-smokers outnumber smokers by about two to one. Of those over 16, about 38 per cent of men smoke and 33 per cent of women.

There are nearly 10 million ex-smokers, according to Action on Smoking and Health (ASH), the anti-smoking organization. Between 1980 and 1982 about a million people gave up smoking.

The proportion of adult cigarette smokers has been decreasing since the early 1970s. In the ten years up to the end of 1982 the proportion of adult male smokers fell by more than a quarter and women by about a fifth. Until 1976 smokers were in a majority in the adult population.

Some 100,000 premature deaths each year appear to be tobacco-related. It is what the Royal College of Physicians calls the 'hidden holocaust'. One estimate is that out of 1,000 young men who smoke in Britain one will be murdered, six will die in road accidents and 250 will die prematurely as a result of smoking.

In 1981 about a third of total deaths from lung cancer were in people below 65.

A quarter of deaths from coronary heart disease appear to be tobacco related, according to Department of Health estimates. ASH calculates that at least 19,000 preventable deaths occur in men and women from this cause.

Method

1 There is quite a lot of information to absorb; read it through carefully once.
2 Read it again, this time taking brief notes for your piece.
3 Decide which arguments against smoking you particularly want to stress.
4 Prepare an outline of the piece.
5 Write the piece, then check it over for inaccuracies.
6 Check your answer against the sample answer. (Do not worry if the content is different, as long as the structure, tone and language are similar.)

Sample answer to *Arguing: example 2*

Mabel Tomkins' statement about her smoking habits illustrates the difficulties many people have in trying to give up the smoking habit. She talks about her dependency on smoking and argues that without cigarettes she has emotional and weight problems. Her argument that lung cancer will probably never happen to her is a very shaky one when we know that 100 000 early deaths a year are caused by diseases related to smoking.

There is no doubt that smokers' determination to give up smoking is the most important factor in success or failure. Most seem unable to give up because of their need for nicotine. Other, less dependent smokers smoke on social occasions. Treatment centres to help smokers give up can hope for a smallish percentage success rate. Drugs and tobacco substitutes have not proved successful, although the prospects for nicotine chewing gum look far more promising. There is a strong argument for this to be supplied on prescription on the National Health Service. I believe the cost of such treatments would be off-set by the huge savings made by treating fewer patients who have diseases caused by smoking.

Lung cancer and heart diseases are very often closely linked with smoking. The argument that 'it will never happen to me' was no doubt used by a large proportion of the 100 000 people who died prematurely last year. An encouraging sign is that cigarette sales have fallen rapidly over the last few years as the medical evidence has grown stronger. There is now no real defence for smoking; it does kill and it is a habit that can be kicked if the smoker is determined enough.

Another hopeful statistic is that non-smokers now outnumber smokers by two to one. ASH, the anti-smoking organisation, reports that millions have given up the fatal habit.

Arguing: example 3
'Capital punishment'
Study the comments below and then discuss some of the points raised. By adding points of your own, develop your argument about the rights and wrongs of capital punishment.

'An eye for an eye, a tooth for a tooth – that's what the Bible says. If someone kills another human being, then he or she should forfeit his or her own life.' (A minister of religion)

'Statistics clearly show that capital punishment is not a deterrent. Whether a society retains the death penalty for murder or not makes absolutely no difference to the number of homicides that occur.' (A lawyer)

'Capital punishment is a deterrent to all except the small minority of criminals who will stop at nothing in the pursuance of crime. Life sentences do not carry the same deterrent effect, especially as so few life sentences are served fully. We must have capital punishment to protect the police and prison officers who have to deal with violent criminals.' (A police inspector)

'No society has the right to take any citizen's life whatever he or she has done. Murder is a horrendous crime, but capital punishment is merely legalised murder.' (Member of anti-capital punishment pressure group)

'I think capital punishment should be reinstated for some crimes such as killing a police officer or terrorist acts. Desperate men and women should be dealt with in a ruthless manner, otherwise terrorist acts will destroy our community.' (6th former)

Method
1 Weigh up all the statements carefully.
2 Extract the points you want to use in your argument.
3 Make sure you deal with 'for' and 'against' arguments, whichever side you are arguing for.
4 Use your notes to draw up an outline for your piece.
5 Remember to write in paragraphs and to use them to develop your argument.
6 Try to link your paragraphs together.
7 Have an effective *opening* and a definite *closing*.
8 Check for all inaccuracies.

Arguing: example 4

'Abortion'

Study the comments below on abortion and discuss some of the points raised. By adding points of your own, develop your argument about the rights and wrongs of abortion.

'Human life is sacrosanct. Only God has the right to give and take away life. Once life has begun in the womb, then no one has the right to take that life away, whatever the circumstances. Abortion is no better than murder.' (Anti-abortion campaigner)

'A woman's right to control her own reproductive process is uppermost. After all, whether to have a child or not is one of the most important decisions a woman has to make in her life. Men make the laws in our society but they do not bear the children. They have no right to tell women what to do about birth. If men did have babies, abortion would have been legalised years ago.' (Pro-abortion campaigner)

'There are too many unwanted children born. The birth of another child living in poverty can bring, not joy, but despair. An illegitimate child born to a teenage girl can shape that young person's future before she has the capacity to make up her mind about the course of her life. Too often, unwanted children are born into unhappiness. For this reason, I give my unenthusiastic but resigned support to abortion rights for women.' (Social worker)

'Everyone has the right to live. The rights of unborn children are just as real as any other individual's rights. Therefore, abortion is a crime against humanity. It is in fact another word for murder.' (An MP)

'In certain cases, such as the possibility of deformed children being born or a woman becoming pregnant by rape, then the abortion of the foetus is justifiable.' (A minister of religion)

'I had a baby when I was sixteen. I was persuaded against having an abortion by my parents and my boy friend. Although I love my child, his birth undoubtedly changed my life and I resent that in many ways. I often think I should have had an abortion.' (Teenage girl)

'Young girls who have unwanted, illegitimate children can have their babies adopted if they so wish, thereby bringing happiness to couples who cannot have children of their own.' (Doctor)

You may be given lists of figures or charts to extract information from and reorganise in a particular form.

Below are lists of best-selling books for a particular week. They are the 'Top Ten' lists for books in three categories.

You have been asked by a local radio station to report briefly on each of the three categories. You are to report on the main changes in the three lists: which books have risen in the lists, which have fallen and which are appearing for the first time. You may also use your judgement to comment on any other relevant facts arising from the information supplied in the lists. Your report should be clear and concise. Note carefully what the heading says about the meaning of the figures in brackets and the 'final' figures.

BEST SELLERS

Figures in brackets give last week's position; final figures indicate number of previous appearances in listings.

PAPERBACKS

1	(6)	A Passage to India	E. M. Forster	Penguin	4
2	(–)	The Danger	Dick Francis	Pan	0
3	(2)	The Secret Diary of Adrian Mole aged 13¾	Sue Townsend	Methuen	70
4	(9)	The Brotherhood	Stephen Knight	Granada	5
5	(7)	Deep Six	Clive Cussler	Sphere	2
6	(1)	Heretics of Dune	Frank Herbert	NEL	2
7	(8)	Blott on the Landscape	Tom Sharpe	Pan	6
8	(–)	The Diamond Waterfall	Pamela Haines	Fontana	0
9	(–)	Scents	Johanna Kingsley	Bantam	3
10	(4)	The Kingdom by the Sea	Paul Theroux	Penguin	3

HARDBACK FICTION

1	(1)	The Growing Pains of Adrian Mole	Sue Townsend	Methuen	32
2	(2)	The Tenth Man	Graham Greene	Bodley Head	1
3	(3)	A Dinner of Herbs	Catherine Cookson	Heinemann	4
4	(6)	If Tomorrow Comes	Sidney Sheldon	Collins	5
5	(–)	The Fall of Kelvin Walker	Alisdair Gray	Canongate	0
6	(4)	The Complete Yes Minister	Johnathan Lynn and Antony Jay	BBC	17
7	(9)	The Bear's Tears	Craig Thomas	M. Joseph	2
8	(5)	Hotel du Lac	Anita Brookner	Cape	24
9	(8)	Field of Blood	Gerald Seymour	Collins	1
10	(10)	The Fourth Protocol	Frederick Forsyth	Hutchinson	25

HARDBACK GENERAL

1	(1)	Mountbatten: The Official Biography	**Philip Ziegler**	Collins	1
2	(2)	In Search of the Trojan War	**Michael Wood**	BBC	5
3	(3)	George Thomas, Mr Speaker: The Memoirs of Viscount Tonypandy		Century	4
4	(–)	The Last Place on Earth	**Roland Huntford**	Pan	2
5	(7)	The Day the Universe Changed	**James Burke**	BBC	1
6	(–)	Galina	**Galina Vishnevskaya**	Hodder	0
7	(4)	Blizzard's Wizard Woodwork	**Richard Blizzard**	BBC	4
8	(5)	Fellwalking with Wainwright	**A. Wainwright Illus Derry Brabbs**	M. Joseph	25
9	(9)	What They Don't Teach You at Harvard Business School	**Mark McCormack**	Collins	20
10	(6)	Television	**Francis Wheen**	Century	2

Method

1 Note that no restriction on the number of words you can use is mentioned, but your report should be concise: your producer would expect a brief report on each category, but would not want to devote a great deal of time to each.
2 He or she would want the essential points summarised; therefore, look out for important changes in the lists and comment on them.
3 Note these down as you read through the lists.
4 Prepare brief outlines for the three sections.
5 Write your report, then check it through again, making sure you haven't missed out important details and have not wasted words.

Sample answer

Paperbacks

'A Passage to India' has leapt to number one position from its previous week's sixth position while 'The Secret Diary of Adrian Mole aged 13¾', in its seventeenth week in the list, has dropped to number three. The most important change is that Dick Francis's 'The Danger' has gone straight to number two in its first week in the list. The other newcomer is 'The Diamond Waterfall' at number eight, whilst 'Scents' reappears at number 9. Last week's leader 'Heretics of Dune' has fallen to number 6.

Hardback Fiction

'The Growing Pains of Adrian Mole' leads the list in its thirty-third week, whilst 'The Tenth Man' retains its second position from last week. 'The Fall of Kelvin Walker' has zoomed up to number 5 on its first appearance whilst 'Hotel du Lac' and 'The Fourth Protocol', after many weeks in the list, look like disappearing at last. 'The Complete Yes Minister', although dropping to sixth position, notches up its eighteenth week in the list.

Hardback General

'Mountbatten' stays at number one for the second week and 'In Search of the Trojan War' and 'George Thomas: Mr Speaker' retain second and third positions respectively. 'The Last Place on Earth' has re-entered at number 4 and 'Galina', in its first listing, arrives at six. 'Fellwalking' after twenty-five weeks shows signs of dropping out of the Top Ten, but 'What They Don't Teach You at Harvard Business School' hangs on at nine after twenty weeks in the best-seller list. 'Television' on its third appearance has dropped from sixth to tenth place.

Examiner's comments:

Format and content: Report written in three sections as requested using the headings of the lists. Deals adequately with each of the lists, commenting on important changes and how long some titles have been in the list.

Expression: Manages to avoid monotonous repetition, which is a danger in this kind of summarising exercise.

Tone and language appropriate for the radio context and audience – fairly formal but with some imaginative vocabulary: 'zoomed', 'notches up', 'hangs on': all these are very acceptable in this context. Some mature vocabulary: 'respectively'.

Accuracy: no errors.

Attempt one or more of the topics below and then check your answers with the sample answers that follow.

1   As you have been an active member of an after-school club activity (e.g. a sports activity, music, drama or dance, chess club) you are asked to write an article about the club for a school publication that will be sent to new pupils to the school. Your article is intended to give new pupils a clear idea of the activities of the club you belong to, and to attract new members. It should not be more than 200 words long.

2   You have been asked to describe in simple, clear terms how to carry out *one* of the following tasks:
      how to decorate a bedroom;
      how to use a video recorder;
      how to make a favourite main course dish.
    Your advice is to be printed in a booklet of 'handy, practical ideas' to be distributed among people of your own age at a community centre. It should be no longer than 200 words.

3   You have been asked to submit a report to a committee of an organisation to which you belong on the possibility of organising a day trip for members. You have to make a recommendation about a possible place to visit, explaining the reasons for going there, transport arrangements, meals and overall cost. Your report may be divided into separate sections but it must make a definite recommendation. It should not be longer than 200 words.

Sample answers
1   *The Drama Club*
    The Drama Club meets after school every Tuesday in the main school hall. When a school production is being rehearsed, then the cast, a large proportion of whom usually belong to the Drama Club, are expected to attend at least twice a week after school. I always look forward to this activity.

    Usually we work on an improvisation. For example, one week, the teacher, or the pupils, might choose the theme of the circus for improvisation work. During the hour-and-a-half we will try to recreate the excitement of the circus ring with clowns, animals, jugglers, speciality acts and all the fun of the circus. We will improvise circus costumes and the teacher will have arranged for suitable music to be on hand to add atmosphere. By the end of the session, we would hope to have worked up some kind of performance.

    Membership is free to all pupils. This next school year we are looking for lots of new members. A production of the musical 'Oliver' is planned for the summer term. Why not come along after school on

Tuesdays? I can promise you an enjoyable time and you will also be learning something.

2 *How to use a video recorder*

Most people use a video recorder to record television programmes while they are out, or to record a programme on one channel while they are watching another. The central point to grasp about video recorders is that they are basically television receivers without a monitor, i.e. they pick up the television signal but cannot actually show the signal being transformed into a live picture.

Most models have a timer device which allows you to set the machine to switch on automatically at certain times to record particular programmes. The best models allow you to set the recorder for up to eight programmes over a period of fourteen days, switching channels automatically according to your settings. This is very useful when you are on holiday and you do not want to miss your favourite programmes.

It is important that your video recorder is well-tuned. You have to select a video channel on your monitor through which you show your recordings. You also have to tune your video recorder channels exactly on the video recorder itself. If you do not do this, your recordings will be unwatchable. Provided you follow basic instructions, video recorders are surprisingly easy to operate.

3 *Report*

My recommendation is that we organise a day trip to Boulogne on a Saturday during July. We could travel by train from Charing Cross to Dover, then cross the Channel by boat to Boulogne. We could leave at 9 a.m. and return by eight in the evening.

The attractions of a day trip to Boulogne are many. There will be opportunities to shop in the hypermarket where many French products such as wines and cheeses are on sale at very attractive prices. We will be able to visit the old section of the town with its many interesting ancient buildings. A bonus will be the splendid meal we will enjoy at any one of the numerous excellent restaurants in Boulogne. Apart from the hypermarket, there are many other shops where members will be able to purchase French goods.

Price reductions are available for the train and sea crossing for groups of ten and above. The basic cost will be £26 but this does not include the cost of meals and any extras. Many of our members have not been abroad before and a day trip to Boulogne will be a pleasant introduction to the Continent. A passport is not required.

Further topics

1 You have been helping to run a 'tuck shop' during breaks at your school. The head of the school asks you to write a report of not more than 200 words about the running of the tuck shop during the previous year, mentioning profits and losses, the behaviour of pupils, the location of the shop, the problem of litter and any other point you think it is important to mention.

2 Pupils have been complaining about the quality and variety of school meals available in your school. As a member of the school council you have been asked to write a report in not more than 250 words about the complaints and to make suggestions for improving the meals. Your report is to be presented to the Parent-Teacher Association.

3 A youth organisation to which you belong has arranged a holiday for a party of foreign young people. You have been asked by the committee of the organisation to write a report about places of interest in the local area which the party could visit. Your report should take cost, travelling time and suitability into account and should not be longer than 250 words.

Understanding and response

You will be tested on your understanding and response to passages of printed material. You may have to take an examination paper, or, alternatively, you may have to produce a folder of course work under the heading of 'Understanding', 'Understanding and Expression' or 'Understanding and Response'.

Questions on the given material will be of various kinds. You will certainly be expected to do more than just extract information from the passage(s). You may well be asked to express a personal response to the passage. You may be asked to make some kind of deduction from the information supplied in the passage. You may be asked to write expressively on a theme arising from the passage. Examples of these types of questions and tasks have been included in the chapter that follows.

The given material

The 'given' material may be a continuous piece of prose or two passages of prose on a similar theme; a poem or poems; an extract from a play. Prose material may be narrative, imaginative, factual, personal accounts, newspaper reports, descriptive or argumentative pieces.

If the material is fictional, it may be a complete short story, or extracts from stories or novels. For the coursework folder, you may be asked to write a response to (at least) one complete book.

You may be presented with newspaper reports of the same events and asked to compare them from the point of view of the opinions expressed, the selection of detail and the use of biased or slanted language.

You may be given a poem or poems and asked questions that test your understanding of the theme and language.

You may be given an extract from a play and asked questions about the content, theme, language and characters.

What the questions will test

The main aim of papers and course work called 'Understanding' is to test your ability to understand and appreciate language in various ways. Below is a guideline to the kind of questions you are likely to get.

1 *Information*: questions will test your ability to extract information from the material and to write answers in your own words as far as possible. For example: 'In paragraph one of the passage, what do we learn about Mrs Smith and . . . ?'

2 *Meaning*: explaining the meaning of words or phrases in the context of the given material. (Read what we have to say about the use of dictionaries on pages xii and 1.) For example: 'What does the phrase "the apple of her eye" (line 26) mean in the context of the passage?'

3 *Figurative language*: really the same type of question as 2, but testing your ability to understand use of non-literal language, e.g. in the form of metaphors, similes or figures of speech. For example: 'Explain the meaning of the simile "The rain like manna from heaven".'

4 *Summarising or re-organising material*: you may be asked to look at particular sections of the given material and to make a summary in your own words of the content or to express the ideas, arguments or facts in your own way.

5 *Appreciation*: testing your ability to appreciate particular uses of language or style (e.g. humorous, persuasive, suspense) or the intention of a writer in a particular piece. You may also be asked to compare two passages. You could also be asked to put yourself in the position of the characters or people in the passage(s).

6 *Inference*: this means 'reading between the lines'. Sometimes writers do not state something outright but imply or indicate what the reader should infer. You are likely to be tested on your ability to pick up these implications or suggestions.

Reading time

In an exam you may be given a separate reading time to read the given material before you are allowed to start answering the questions. Use that time to the full.

If you are allowed to take notes during the reading time, do so in short, concise phrases.

Read the material through two or three times. Do not sit staring into space or gazing round to see what your pals are doing.

Answering the questions

Make sure you know what the point of each question is. Watch out for questions that direct you to particular sections of the material and limit your answer to that section. For example: 'How do we know from paragraph three of the passage that Anne was extremely embarrassed by her situation?' Answers to this question should only focus on the third paragraph.

Answer all questions, unless you are given a choice.

Most exam papers of this kind will have the number of marks awarded to each question printed in brackets at the end of the questions, e.g. (6) or (4). If the figure (10) appears at the end of one question and (4) at the end of another, then this will give you a strong hint that the question attracting ten marks requires a much longer answer than the question attracting only four marks.

If you find you are repeating material in an answer that you have already used in answering another question, then this will almost certainly be because you have missed the point of one of the questions. Check again what you are being asked and, if necessary, start the answer again by scoring out neatly what you have already written.

Extract: *Beyond the Dragon's Mouth*

You may be given an extract from an autobiography to read and then have to answer questions on it. Below there is a passage from Shiva Naipaul's autobiography, *Beyond the Dragon's Mouth*, in which he describes his arrival in London from Trinidad in the 1960s. Answer the questions before checking your answer against the sample answers that are given.

I was nineteen years old when I left Trinidad to come as a student to England. For a few days immediately after I arrived I stayed with my brother in a hotel in Blackheath. The hotel was inhabited chiefly by the middle-aged and solitary. Memories are tinged with the semi-magical quality which invests the week of my arrival: the impression of fantasy – of unreal things happening in an unreal world – was strong.

But the magic soon faded. The polite rituals of the hotel functioned in a void. I began to feel isolated in Blackheath. It seemed an infinity away from what I fondly imagined to be the centre of things. Where

10 that was I had no clear idea. Neither could I say with any certainty what I expected to find when I got there. The pink glow kindling the sky nightly promised adventure. I wished to draw closer to the fiery source producing it. The Big City was beckoning.

Finally I saw a room advertised at a price I could afford. I rang the number supplied. It turned out to be an accommodation agency. Was the room they had advertised still available? Unfortunately, no. However – the lady's voice tinkled encouragingly at the other end of the line – they had several like it on their books. Why did I not come to their office?

20 The office, a cramped cubicle approached up a tortuous flight of stairs, was on the Earl's Court Road. A wiry woman in a luminously red cardigan was in charge. I introduced myself.

'Ah! so you are the foreign gentleman who rang earlier.' Her voice had shed its telephonic twinkle. But it was not unfriendly. 'Come in and have a seat and we shall see what we can do for you. We have managed to fix up quite a few coloured people in our time.' She moved briskly to a paper-cluttered desk and sat down. 'Now you say you can't afford more than five pounds a week . . .'

'Maximum,' I said quickly.

30 'Quite, quite . . . mmmm.' She thumbed through a box of index cards.

'Student?' she enquired absently after a while.

'Yes.'

'Studying what?'

I told her. The words sounded impossibly big and foolish.

'Really!' Extracting an index card she frowned thoughtfully at it.

She reached for the telephone and dialled. 'Some of these landlandies are a bit fussy when it comes to . . .'

She reverted to her telephonic twinkle. 'Hello. Is that Mrs . . . ? This is the – Accommodation Agency here. I've got a young foreign student who's looking for a room. He seems a nice quiet fellow. What's that? Yes, I'm afraid he is. But . . . no, no. Not at all. Of course I understand.' 40

The receiver clicked down. She considered me. 'Next time I think we'll say straight off that you come from India. It's better not to beat about the bush, don't you agree? Anyway some of them don't mind Indians so much.'

'But I don't come from India.'

'You don't?' She stared at me. 'But you look Indian.'

'Well, I am Indian. But I was born in the West Indies.' 50

'The West Indies?' She seemed vaguely aghast.

This was my initiation in the sub-world of 'racial prejudice'. I had read and heard about it at home: nearly everyone who had been to England had his own cautionary tale to tell. Now it was happening to me and I could not quite bring myself to believe in it.

I waited while the lady dialled number after number '. . . I've got a young Indian student here who is looking for a room . . .' Her eyes were clouding with exhaustion, I stopped listening. Then, out of the blue: 'Yes. Yes. As I said, he seems a nice quiet type. I shall send him round straight away. He's right here with me in the office.' She put the 60 receiver down and regarded me with an air of triumph. 'I told you we could fix you up. Didn't I?'

SAMPLE QUESTIONS AND ANSWERS

1　Why did the writer have 'an impression of fantasy' (line 5) during his first week in London? (6)
2　'The pink glow kindling the sky nightly promised adventure' (line 11). Explain in your own words what this sentence means to you. (6)
3　Summarise in your own words the telephone conversation between the writer and the lady at the accommodation agency. (8)
4　'Her voice had shed its telephonic twinkle' (line 23). What does this sentence suggest about the woman's manner? (5)
5　Explain in your own words what happens when the woman from the agency makes the first telephone call. (6)
6　What confusion arises between the writer and the woman about his coming from India? (4)
7　'I could not quite bring myself to believe in it' (line 55). What is it the writer could not quite believe in? (6)
8　How do we know from the last paragraph that the woman had difficulty in finding accommodation for the writer? (6)
9　Express in your own words what your reaction to this account is – where your sympathies lie, whether you think this account is 'true-to-life' and any other point you may want to write about. (12)

119 *Autobiography*

Qu. 1 It was his first week in a new country that was very different from where he came from. Everything seemed unreal, as though he were cut off from the real world, and this impression was helped by the lonely feeling Blackheath and the hotel gave him and the fact that he was so far away from the centre of the city.

Qu. 2 The glow of the lights from the centre of London seemed to symbolise the adventures the big city held in store for him. Somehow they were outside, looking at promised excitement from afar.

Qu. 3 First of all, the advertised room had already gone. There is perhaps a suggestion that the advert had been a 'come-on', a ploy to get people to phone the agency to begin with. The lady's voice was friendly and very helpful and she was quick to point out that they had lots of similar accommodation available.

Qu. 4 It suggests that now the writer had turned up at the agency the woman's manner was less welcoming, as the customer had taken the bait.

Qu. 5 The woman tries to 'sell' the writer to the landlady as a 'nice quiet fellow' but is obviously asked whether he's coloured or not. When she learns that he is Indian, the landlady turns him down. The agency woman remains polite to the landlady and seems to accept it as quite a normal occurrence.

Qu. 6 She doesn't seem to be able to understand that, although he is Indian, he does not come from India but from the West Indies.

Qu. 7 He could not quite bring himself to believe that racial prejudice existed in England. People from his own country had told him about it but here he was experiencing it for himself.

Qu. 8 She had to dial 'number after number'. Her eyes became 'clouded with exhaustion' until 'out of the blue' she was able to find him somewhere. The impression is that it took many calls to get a positive response.

Qu. 9 My sympathies are with the writer, especially as he was young, new to the country and in a big city. He was facing racial prejudice for the first time and the woman's manner, although in some ways she was helpful, was rather patronising. It cannot be easy to accept that you are the victim of racial prejudice. It seems a very true account of a sad experience. I also like the way the writer describes his feelings of anticipation about the city. There is a sadness and truth about the writing. The writer is communicating an experience that he has felt deeply.

Notes **1** Requires careful reading, or reading between the lines. **2** Notice the 'in your own words'. **3** Must summarise in your own words. **4** You must deduce something from the passage here. *Interpreting* the meaning. **5** *Summarising* a section of the passage. **6** Straight explanation **7** Straightforward analysis of meaning. **8** Asking for evidence from passage. **9** An open-ended question for you to give your own response. Notice 12 marks awarded, so longer answer is required.

Extract: *Bird lovers*
You could be presented with a newspaper article dealing with a particular issue and/or event. Below is an article that gives an account of conflict between 'naturalists' or 'conservationists' – people anxious about preserving natural resources and animal life – and the inhabitants of a small Scottish island.

Bird lovers brave
Islay's wrath again

The battle of Duich Moss will be resumed this week when naturalists from Friends of the Earth return unbowed to the Scottish island of Islay to plead again the cause of the white-fronted goose.

On Monday, Friends of the Earth, led by David Bellamy, were booed off the island by local people more 0 interested in jobs than geese.

The row has focused attention on an increasingly acrimonious conflict between conservationists and those who feel that protecting the environment should come second to protecting jobs.

Residents of Islay claim that the campaign by 'English outsiders' to save Duich Moss, the winter habitat 0 of 600 rare geese, could threaten local whisky distillery jobs and halt 1,500 years of domestic peatcutting.

Friends of the Earth are attempting to reverse a decision by George Younger, the Scottish secretary, giving permission to Scottish Malt Distillers to drain part of Duich Moss so that peat can be extracted for malt whisky production. The moss is an 0 official site of special scientific interest.

The naturalists say the distillers could use an alternative site and that no jobs are threatened. They believe they have been the victims of a scurrilous and well-organised campaign by local 'environment bashers'.

Donnie McKerrell, a local councillor, said: 'If we don't stop them in their tracks at Duich Moss they'll take over the whole of Islay. There are already 10 sites of special scientific interest on the island. In my opinion 10 that's 10 too many. The people of Islay are fed up being told what they should do by outsiders, and if they come back here next week they'll get exactly the same reception.'

McKerrell has been accused by Jonathan Porritt, director of Friends of the Earth, of recruiting a vigilante group from Islay pubs to harass the naturalists in their campaign. 20

Friends of the Earth say that all they want is a two-year moratorium on peat-cutting while a survey of its effect on the habitat is carried out.

The birds consume huge quantities of grass planted by local beef and dairy farmers for silage. One local farmer said: 'The fact is the bloody birds eat everybody's grass and not just the stuff in the protected sites. 30 But so far nobody has worked out a way of teaching geese to read conservationists' maps.'

SAMPLE QUESTIONS AND ANSWERS

1 According to the first paragraph, who or what are the naturalists defending? (2)
2 Explain how the campaign to save Duich Moss has brought the naturalists into conflict with the islanders. (8)
3 What do the naturalists say about the issue of jobs for the islanders? (4)
4 Summarise in your own words the local councillor's arguments. (6)
5 What has the councillor been accused of by the director of Friends of the Earth? Use your own words as far as possible. (4)
6 Explain in your own words what Friends of the Earth want. (4)
7 What are the islanders' attitude to the birds? (6)
8 What is your own response to the topics raised by this article about the conflict? Whose side are you on – the conservationists or the islanders? (8)

Qu. 1 The white-fronted goose.

Qu. 2 The islanders are very concerned about the jobs produced for the island by the local distillery, which has been given permission to drain part of Duich Moss where 600 rare geese live in winter. Peat is extracted from the moss. The naturalists are concerned about the effect of the draining and peat extraction on the rare birds and on the site which is designated as being of special scientific interest.

Qu. 3 The naturalists claim that their defence of the site need not threaten jobs, as an alternative site for the peat extraction could be used.

Qu. 4 McKerrell, a local councillor, is worried that Duich Moss is just the first stage in the naturalists' campaign to take over the whole island because there are ten sites of scientific interest on the island. He claims that the islanders resent being ordered about by outsiders.

Qu. 5 He has been accused of organising groups of people from the pub and encouraging them to take action against the naturalists in an attempt to hinder their work.

Qu. 6 They want a two-year ban on peat-cutting while an investigation of the effect it has is in progress. They want to find out if it will harm the winter home of the geese.

Qu. 7 The islanders do not like the birds much because they eat large amounts of grass planted by local farmers. One local farmer sums up their feelings by pointing out that the geese eat grass all over the island, not just on the protected sites.

Qu. 8 My sympathies in this conflict are almost equally divided between the islanders and the naturalists. The islanders may well feel outsiders are pushing their noses into their business and trying to thwart attempts to bring more jobs to the island. However, the argument by the naturalists that there is an alternative site for the peatcutting, if true, seems worth considering. The local councillor seems rather insular and very distrustful of outsiders. There is no one right or wrong in this situation.

Notes **1** Straightforward extraction of information – a phrase will do as answer. **2** *Summarising* the relevant sections in your own words as far as possible. **3** Again *extracting* information and *rewording*. **4** *Summarising* direct speech in your own words. **5** *Extracting information* and rewording. **6** Use dictionary for difficult words. **7** *Summarising* in own words. **8** *Personal response* – express opinions, balance arguments; develop your answer. The above answer is only intended as a guide – you could take quite a different line.

Extract: *British Summer*

Below is another newspaper article. This time the subject is one British summer. Read it carefully and then answer the questions that follow. Notice that the last question asks you to write expressively. Write your answers to the questions before checking them against the model answers and the notes.

Eastbourne woke up yesterday to another rainswept, chilly morning – and the surprise news that it is the sunniest resort in Britain so far this summer.

The official sunshine figures for this soggy summer are being amassed at the Bracknell Weather Centre for the purely academic exercise of nominating the one place in Britain where holidaymakers will get less soaked than anywhere else.

At the south coast resort the sun eventually broke through after the morning's downpour.

It rained and rained on this South Coast resort for most of last week. Tourists took coach tours and refused to emerge from their coaches. Only the foreigners wear shorts: only they have suntans.

On the beach, four Italian students venture into the water, shoes off and trousers rolled up in the English way. At home it is 40°C in the shade; in Eastbourne 17°C.

Maria Azzollini said: 'Our English books keep talking about the weather. Now I understand why.'

No English were to been seen bathing, even English-style, at Eastbourne yesterday. Indeed, the only person on the beach by the pier was a man in a raincoat with a metal detector.

The Met Office charts on Eastbourne's seafront give away the secret. Last Sunday there were four hours of sun. There were also 25 millimetres of rain.

'It was atrocious,' Len Joyce, of Enfield, recalls. He is another of the 1·3m visitors to Eastbourne each year.

One Eastbourne attraction is the Butterfly Centre, where 500 exotic butterflies, such as the Camberwell Beauty from south-east London, dart about in 5,000 sq ft of tropical gardens. Last week, however, there was a crisis and the heating had to be turned up. With no sun the butterflies stopped flying.

Yesterday they fluttered as usual, conned into believing it is summer by a 600,000 btu gas boiler.

'People have come here on holiday and left after two or three days,' said Geoffrey Goodall, a partner in the centre. 'If I were at a hotel in Eastbourne I would not move out of the bar.'

The sunniest place in Britain? 'Not at the moment unfortunately,' said Sandra Friedberg, 21, of the resort's tourist centre. 'I haven't seen any sun for three or four days. Two people came in the office today and they were really brown. I said, "Where did you get that tan?" They said they'd been sitting on the seafront when it wasn't raining and they'd got it from the wind.'

The Bracknell centre experts said Britain is simply enjoying a near-normal summer. The only reason it seems so miserable is that the country has been spoiled by recent unnaturally fine summers. The centre can even produce figures to prove it.

SAMPLE QUESTIONS AND ANSWERS

1   'For the purely academic exercise of nominating the one place in Britain' (paragraph 2). What does the phrase 'the purely academic exercise' mean in this context?   (3)
2   'Where holidaymakers will get less soaked than anywhere else' (paragraph 2). What does this tell us about the weather this particular year?   (4)
3   Why had the reporter chosen to go to Eastbourne for this report?   (3)
4   Why do you think only the foreigners had suntans?   (4)
5   What does the Italian student mean when she says that now she understood why the weather was mentioned so often in English books?   (4)
6   'Bathing, even English-style' (paragraph 6). How is this described in another part of the article?   (3)
7   How many visitors come to Eastbourne each year?   (2)
8   Explain in your own words as far as possible the crisis that occurred at the Butterfly Centre.   (8)
9   Explain how two holidaymakers had acquired a suntan.   (6)
10 Summarise in your own words what the Bracknell Weather Centre had to say about the summer.   (8)
11 Imagine you are a holidaymaker in Eastbourne for a week during this rainy summer. Write a holiday postcard to a friend, using not more than 100 words, describing the holiday you are having. You may use details from the article if you like.   (12)

Qu. 1   The task is being carried out just for the sake of doing it, not for any particular purpose.

Qu. 2   The use of the words 'less soaked' tells us that it is more a matter of finding out which resort had less rain than the others, rather than which had the most sun. In other words, it is an atrocious summer.

Qu. 3   The Meteorological Office at Bracknell had stated Eastbourne had had more sun during the summer than any other place in Britain, so in reporting on the British summer the reporter had gone there to find out for himself and to test the local reactions.

Qu. 4   The foreigners obviously have suntans acquired in their own country before they came on holiday to Britain.

Qu. 5   She had been puzzled why people in English books mentioned the weather so often; now she realised that they did so because it was so unbelievably bad.

Qu. 6   'Bathing, even English-style' means wading into the water with the shoes off and the trousers rolled up.

Qu. 7   1·3 million visitors come to Eastbourne each year.

Qu. 8   The absence of sun, and therefore warmth, meant that the exotic butterflies did not flutter about, so the visitors could not see them. The heating, via a gas boiler, had to be turned up and the butterflies started flying again.

Qu. 9   They had sat on the seafront during a period when rain wasn't falling and the wind had tanned their faces.

Qu. 10   They stated that it was an average summer. Statistics showed that the summer was normal for this country, but that people had been misled by recent very good summers which had made them forget the usual British summer.

Qu. 11   Yes, I have to mention it – the weather! It is dominating the holiday. I read in the papers that Eastbourne is the sunspot of Britain – well, not this week it isn't! I haven't seen the sun yet but the biting wind may give me a tan. Went to the exotic Butterfly Centre yesterday – even the butterflies had gone on strike! Have gone to the pictures twice, walked by the cliffs, haunted the amusement arcades and despite the cold have eaten too much. Next year the south of France or a week in front of a sun-lamp!

You may be presented with two pieces of expressive writing dealing with the same theme. Questions will centre on your understanding of the language and content of the passages. You may also be asked to write expressively on a theme close to that of the passages.

Extract A   *Pentimento*

Read the following passage which tells of the experience of Lillian Hellman, a writer. Just before the outbreak of the second world war, she is asked to carry money, hidden in a candy box and in a hat that she has to wear, from Austria to Germany; the money is to be used for bribes to get Jews and other victims of the Hitler regime out of the dreaded concentration camps that were already in existence in Germany. The author is travelling by train and sharing a compartment with two young women whom she has never met before.

For the next few hours the three of us dozed or read until the thin girl tapped me on the knee and said we would be crossing the border in five or ten minutes. I suppose everybody comes to fear in a different way, but I have always felt very hot or very cold, and neither has anything to do with the weather. Now, waiting, I was very hot. As the train pulled to a standstill, I got up to go outside – people were already leaving the train to pass through a check gate, and men were coming on the train to inspect baggage in the cars ahead of us – without my coat or my new hat. I was almost out of the compartment door when the thin girl said,
10 'You will need your hat and your coat. It is of a windiness.'

'Thank you. But I'm not cold.'

Her voice changed sharply. 'You will have need of your coat. Your hat is nice on your head.'

I didn't ask questions because the tone in which she spoke was the answer. I turned back, put the coat round my shoulders, put on the hat that felt even heavier now with the wads of something that filled the lining, and let the girls go past me as I adjusted it in the mirror. Coming out on the platform, they were ahead of me, separated from me by several people who had come from other compartments. The thin girl
20 dropped her purse and, as she picked it up, stepped to one side and moved directly behind me. We said nothing as we waited in line to reach the two uniformed men at the check gate. As the man in front of me was having his passport examined, the thin girl said, 'If you have a temporary travel-through visa, it might take many more minutes than others. But that is nothing. Do not worry.'

It didn't take many minutes more than others. I went through as fast as anybody else – turned in a neat line with the other travellers, went back to the train. The thin girl was directly behind me, but as we got to

the steps of the train, she said, 'Please,' and pushed me aside to climb
in first. When we reached our compartment, the fat girl was in her seat 30
listening to two customs men in the compartment next to ours as they
had some kind of good-natured discussion with a man who was
opening the luggage.

The thin girl said, 'They are taking great time with the luggage.' As
she spoke, she leaned over and picked up my candy box. She took off
the ribbon and said, 'Thank you. I am hungry for a chocolate. Most
kind.'

I said, 'Please, please,' and I knew I was never meant for this kind of
thing. 'I am carrying it to a friend for a gift. Please do not open it.' As
the customs men came into our compartment, the thin girl was chewing 40
on a candy, the box open on her lap. I did not know much about the
next few minutes except that all baggage was dragged down from the
racks, that my baggage took longer than the baggage of my companions. I remember the heavy girl chatting away, and something
being said about my travelling visa and how I was going to a theatre
festival because I was a playwright. And the name Hellman came into
the conversation I could only half understand. One of the customs men
said, 'Jew,' and the heavy girl said certainly the name was not always of
a Jew and gave examples of people and places I couldn't follow. Then
the man thanked us, replaced everything neatly, and bowed them- 50
selves out of the door.

Somewhere in the next hours I stopped being hot or cold and was not
frightened again that day. The thin girl had neatly retied my candy box
but I don't think any of us spoke again until the train pulled into the
station. When the porters came for the baggage, I told myself that I
should be nervous, that if the money had been discovered at the border
gate nothing much could have happened because I was still close to
France. Now was the time, therefore, for caution, intelligence, reasonable fears. But it wasn't the time, and I laughed at that side of me that
so often panics at a moment of no consequence, so often grows listless 60
and sleepy near danger.

Extract B *Sumitra's story*
An Asian family have recently come to Britain from Africa. The family
have difficulty in finding a place to live. They are placed in a small hotel by
the local council.

Never had life seemed so bleak, so bare, to Bap and Mai. Living in
the guest house brought them into their first close contact with the
corrupt white culture. Everything evil in Western civilisation seemed
to surround them; unmarried mothers, wives who had been left or
been deserted by their husbands, families arguing violently. Even the
ordinary guests came back late at night, drunk, slamming doors, falling

up the stairs, swearing loudly, vomiting. Raucous laughter rang out.
Bap left the house early each morning to walk wearily to the bus-stop,
to wait beneath the daubed message: PAKIS GO HOME! His life was
10   in ruins – he could not provide his family with a proper home and felt
that his work was beneath him. His earning power, his morale, his
self-respect was threatened.

Mai stayed in her room all day, too ill and depressed to learn the new
language. When Ela and Bimla returned from school she took them to
Leela's house. There she felt safe. She knew what was expected of her,
did not have to struggle and strain with each word. The children played
with Trupti, Leela's baby. When all the family had arrived back from
school or work, they would eat in an island of peace, a haven from
which they had to set off each evening, back to the alien ground. Bap
20   and Mai were frightened by the hostility they could sense. So they
clung to their own customs, their own traditions. They lived on one
side of the hotel and Jean lived on the other and between them was this
great gulf of fear. 'This fear is concentrated on me,' Sumitra thought to
herself, 'Jean is telling me to go away, and Mai is telling me to stay
beside her. Yet I cannot do either. I will have to grow up and live my
own life.'

SAMPLE QUESTIONS AND ANSWERS
Section A   Answer all the questions
1   'I suppose everybody comes to fear in a different way.' (line 3 of Passage
    A). What do you think the writer means by this?   (3)
2   From the way she speaks how can you detect that the thin girl does not
    speak English as her first language?   (5)
3   In Passage A, how do we, and the 'I' of the passage, gradually come to
    learn that the two girls are involved in the intrigue?   (8)
4   How does the writer explain her lack of fear when the train arrives at the
    station?   (5)
5   Explain in your own words why the family felt so unhappy in the guest
    house.   (8)
6   The author of Passage B has used some figurative language to express
    her meaning. Here is an example; explain what the writer means, paying
    particular attention to the words in italics: 'they would eat in an *island* of
    peace, a *haven* from which they had to set off each evening, back to the
    alien ground.' (lines 18–19)   (6)
7   What themes do you think the two passages have in common?   (6)

Section B   Choose one of the following to write about in prose, poetry or a
playscript. You should write between 300 and 350 words.
1   Describe an occasion when you felt fear because of your surroundings or
    some menace near you. Say what you were doing, and describe your
    thoughts and feelings in detail and make clear what happened at the end.
2   Write a scene from a play in which a young person is involved in keeping
    a secret from an adult or adults.

Section A

Qu. 1 The writer is saying that everyone has his or her own reaction to frightening situations, or his or her own way of dealing with fear.

Qu. 2 She says 'It is of a windiness' instead of 'It is windy'. There is a certain clumsiness or over-formal manner of speaking when she advises the narrator to wear her coat and keep her hat on. A British person would have said something like: 'You'll need your coat. Your hat suits you.' Later she says 'They are taking great time with the luggage' instead of 'a long time'.

Qu. 3 The advice the thin girl gives about the coat and the hat was the first hint, then the way the thin girl deliberately dropped her purse so she had an excuse to be directly behind the author. She also tries to calm the author's nerves by telling her not to worry if she is delayed at the check gate. She goes in front of the author when they return to the train to check things out. The fat girl was listening to the customs men in the next compartment. To make it seem there is nothing in the candy box other than chocolates, the thin girl opens the box and starts eating a chocolate despite the fact that she has not been offered one *and* despite the protests of the narrator. The fat (or 'heavy') girl explains to the customs men that Hellman was not necessarily a Jewish name.

Qu. 4 She explains that, although the arrival at the station was potentially the most dangerous time, she felt no fear because she was often anxious when there was no reason; when she was in real danger she felt indifference and lethargy.

Qu. 5 They seemed to be surrounded by the worst examples of western life: broken families and people being violent. The guests were always getting drunk and behaving badly. Bap felt the guest house was not a suitable house for his family and that he had not the earnings to provide a decent one. They seemed to be surrounded by hostile people. There were racist slogans on the walls and they could sense that people did not like them. Sumitra felt Jean's hostility and thought it was focused on her especially.

Qu. 6 The time they ate their meal together became a safe time in a safe place (a 'haven') cut off from the surrounding hostile world (an 'island') but a place they had to leave to return to a strange and frightening world outside ('alien ground').

Qu. 7 Both passages deal with fear; the first tells of a woman involved in a secret intrigue where she feels very unsure of herself and alone, surrounded by menacing people who are about to discover what she is doing. She is, however, helped by the two girls. In Passage B, the theme is again fear – fear of a hostile world where the only consolation is the family and its unity. Another theme in common is racial prejudice – the customs men and their questions about the narrator being Jewish and the Asian family is the target of racial prejudice as well.

Notes on these answers:

The answers are in the candidate's own words as far as possible; they answer the questions that are asked and only include relevant material; they use material from the passage to back up what they are saying; the lengths of the answers reflect the number of marks awarded to particular questions.

Question 6 asked you to explain the use of figurative language in a sentence from Passage B. Figurative language is language which uses figures of speech such as metaphor, simile, alliteration. *Figurative language* is different to *literal language*. If you say something in a *literal* way, you mean exactly what you say; so, the sentence would mean the family ate *literally* on an island and a haven; the figurative use of the words (metaphors in this example) means the writer is trying to express that to the family it seemed like an island, a haven; it had the qualities of an island, a haven. That is what has been explained in the answer given above.

Section B (Model answer to 2)

(A teacher enters the classroom to find a cartoon of himself drawn on the blackboard. He hides a smile from the pupils and puts on a stern face.)

Teacher: So who's the clever artist, then?
(Silence. He looks round the room.)
Alison? Do you know anything about this?

Alison: No, sir.

Teacher: You're turning red, Alison. Could that be guilt?

Alison: I can't help it. I always look like a beetroot when someone accuses me of something.

Teacher: I know you can draw, Alison.

Alison: That's not my work, sir. It's too flattering. I would have made it a lot more . . .

Teacher: Yes, well, we'll leave that unsaid, shall we? Cyril! How about you? Guilty or not guilty?

Cyril: Not guilty, sir.

Teacher: Come on, Cyril, I didn't come down in the last shower of rain. I know you. This is just your kind of thing.

Cyril: Me, sir? No, sir. You've got me wrong, sir.

Teacher: On the contrary, I've got you very right.

Cyril: Evidence, sir?

Teacher: One – your past record.

Cyril: Cannot be produced in court, sir. That's prejudice, not evidence.

Teacher: Two – you too are good with the old crayon or chalk.

Cyril: Very nice of you to say so, sir.

Teacher: Three – you've got chalk marks on your hands!

Cyril:	Where?
	(He rubs his hands on his jacket.)
	Nice one, sir. But not so, I'm afraid.
Teacher:	Four . . .
Cyril:	Yes, sir?
Teacher:	My strong hunch.
Cyril:	Hunches are not allowed, sir.
Teacher:	This is my classroom so hunches are allowed.
Cyril:	Very undemocratic, sir.
Teacher:	Maybe, but satisfying. So own up! Come clean!
Cyril:	Me, sir?
Teacher:	Yes, *you*, Cyril.
Cyril:	I told you, in this case I am entirely innocent. I grant you in the past I have been guilty of a few minor crimes but this cannot be laid at my doorstep.
Teacher:	But you know who did do it. So who?
Cyril:	Sir! You're asking me to be a supergrass.
Teacher:	Yes!
Cyril:	I can't do that. I could never look myself in the mirror again.
Teacher:	I'm surprised you can anyway.
Cyril:	Unfair, sir.
Teacher:	Granted! Well, it seems the mystery is going to remain unsolved for the moment. But I will find the culprit, believe me . . . And Cyril . . .
Cyril:	Yes, sir?
Teacher:	Wipe it off the board, will you?
Cyril:	Oh, sir . . .

Notes on the sample answer   Note how the playscript is set out: the names of the characters are written at the edge of the paper or in the margin; the words they speak are written opposite. No speech marks are used in playscripts. The actions or reactions of the characters are described within brackets to mark these off from the words they speak. In everyday speech we often do not speak in complete sentences so the speech in this scene reflects that:

Cyril:	Evidence sir?
Teacher:	One – your past record.

Note also how the scene has a definite beginning and a definite end. It starts with the teacher entering the room and is rounded off neatly by the teacher asking Cyril to wipe the board and Cyril's groan.

You will sometimes be asked to read two contrasting accounts or reports of the same event. The questions will test your understanding of the different viewpoints or standpoints presented in the accounts or reports. There might also be opportunities for expressive writing arising out of the passages.

Extract: *Derby Day*

Read the following accounts of *Derby Day* (the day the famous Derby horserace takes place) from the points of view of (A) a stable lad and (B) a bookmaker. Then answer the questions.

Report A

Kevin Parker, nicknamed Nosey with typical racing wit, sleeps like a switched-off ear-trumpet. He does not normally get into Guy Harwood's yard at Pulborough, where he has worked since leaving school 12 years ago, until 7a.m. But on Wednesday he was alert at 6.10 and in the yard twenty minutes later. Not because he had to be – the Sussex village is only an hour's drive from Epsom – but because he was taking Alphabatim, whom he has looked after since the colt first came into training 20 months ago, to run in the Derby.

10 At 8.30 he led the handsome bay down the ramp of Harwood's big buttercup-yellow horsebox, showed his stable servant's pass to the security men clustering round the Epsom stable-gate and introduced Alphabatim to the quiet north-east stable that is reserved for Derby runners.

Nosey then had to plait Alf up. He made neat bunches of the second favourite's mane, but came back later than expected, having 'had a bit of trouble because Alf kept looking out of the stable door'.

At 2.30 Nosey led Alf in his smart cream sheet with scarlet trim round the back of the course and into the saddling enclosure. The colt had his head high, looking round, loving the high-charged

20 atmosphere.

Only when the parade was over did Nosey lose his link with Alf. His colt, and Lester's famous bottom, disappeared towards the start. Nosey had no time to feel alone: he hurried by pre-arrangement to the ITV box above the winner's circle, where he was interviewed by Brough Scott. Brough invited him to watch the race on ITV's set, but Robert Sangster got between Nosey and the screen, and the lad, not liking to intrude, saw only patches of the race.

But he did see that Alf came out of the starting stalls late, and going up the hill had only two behind him. When the pacemakers fell away,

30 he got as near as he ever did, which was to finish fifth.

Even while Secreto took the bows, the fizz went out of the air backstage. In the stable lads' canteen it was just another quiet tea-time with a warm breeze sifting the beech hedge by the stable block. 'I'd given up hope of winning it at the top of the hill,' Nosey said. 'He wanted to be up there. He's better than that. He'll prove himself, he's a good horse.'

Report B

From John White's bookmaking position half a furlong from the finish, it was clear that it was a matter of inches. 'And the difference for me,' said White just after they had passed the post, 'is about £9000.' White thought that El Gran Senor had won, a result that would have meant him losing more than £4000 on the race.

Then they called for a photograph and bookmakers better placed than White were offering 3–1 against El Gran Senor. That made White more optimistic and it also gave him the chance to reduce his risk. Suddenly Tattersall's enclosure was alive with action again, and White, using his tic-tac man to communicate over the heads of the crowd, was betting hard. 10

Just three minutes earlier, when the race began and all eyes were on the far side of the Downs, punters and bookmakers, those natural adversaries, had been strangely in unison, caught in the spell that separates the bedlam of the pre-race betting market and the roaring wave of enthusiasm, and the curses, of the finish.

White stood on his box, peering through his binoculars at the runners. He could do nothing more. Having taken £7000 in bets on the Derby he had closed his money-bag. Most of the bets – 250 in all – had been taken in those last hectic few minutes before the off, when White and his team, working like demons, were in their element. 20

For all their efforts, White had lost on the first two races of the day, both won by the favourites. But when they announced the result of the photograph, White permitted himself a brief smile. All he had to do now was pay out on the handful of bets placed on Secreto. Of course some of his takings had been used in hedging his bets, but the rest was profit.

Then came the bombshell – a stewards' inquiry. Punters held their breath but for White it was a time for action. He started betting again, this time on the result of the enquiry. By the time the announcement came, he had reduced his liabilities on El Gran Senor to £1000. It wouldn't have hurt too much if the stewards had ruled it the winner. As it happened, White ended up counting money, £4,867 in profit, and the punters were tearing up their betting slips. White had won but it was a close-run thing. 30

SAMPLE QUESTIONS AND ANSWERS

1 State where (*a*) Kevin Parker and (*b*) John White watched the race from. (3)
2 Explain in your own words the differences in their involvement in the Derby between the stable lad and the bookmaker. (6)
3 Explain fully why Kevin Parker only saw part of the race. (4)
4 'The fizz went out of the air.' (line 31) What does this tell us about the way the stable lads felt after the race and how does this contrast with the bookmaker's actions after the race had been run? (4)
5 With whom do you have more sympathy – Kevin Parker or John White? Give your reasons using information from the passage. (8)
6 Imagine that either Kevin Parker or John White writes a letter to a friend in which he comments on his experience of Derby Day. Write one of these letters using information from either of the accounts. (20)

Qu. 1 Kevin Parker watched the race from the ITV box; John White from his position where he carried on his bookmaking business a hundred yards from the finishing post.

Qu. 2 The stable lad had a tremendous pride in the horse he looked after and he desperately wanted it to do well. His role was to prepare the horse for the race. The bookmaker's interest was all to do with bets and making a profit. He cared which horse won the race but only because it made a difference to the number of winning bets he would have to pay out on.

Qu. 3 Someone – Robert Sangster – got in his way so he could not see the television set and he was too shy to ask him to move or to get himself a better viewing point.

Qu. 4 The excitement of the race had gone and things fell a bit flat. They had a quiet cup of tea. As a contrast the bookmaker had to continue betting on the result of the enquiry.

Qu. 5 It seems that Nosey got little attention or thanks for his hard work. Even though he is invited to watch the race in the ITV box he feels out of place. Afterwards there is a feeling of anti-climax and disappointment. John White, however, makes a lot of money out of his efforts. His profits depend on the people who bet losing, so I have little sympathy with him. His profits also depend on the hard work of people like Kevin who get all the horses ready for the races.

Qu. 6

11, The Yard,
Pulborough.
10.6.8 –

Dear Joe,

I thought I'd write and tell you about my experiences on Derby Day because I know you're very interested in it. It was certainly a day to remember. It's not every day I get on the telly!

Frankly, it was a mixture of a day – excitement *and* real disappointment. My horse, Alf, did quite well but not nearly as well as he should have done. I put a lot of hard work into preparing him and I really thought he had a good chance of winning. But I don't think he was given much of a chance by the jockey because he came out of the stalls late and was too far behind at the top of the hill to make much headway. After the race I was felt quite down but there was the compensation of being interviewed on the telly by Brough Scott!

After the interview I was invited by Brough to watch the race on the ITV set. Imagine me among all those important people! As it turned out, I didn't see much of the race as someone important got in front of me and you know how polite I am!

Still, all in all, it was a great day and I only hope there will be more exciting Derby Days for me in the future. And a winner too! I hope to see you soon.

Regards,

Kevin

Kevin

Below are two passages; the first is from a writer's account of his own childhood, the second an extract from a novel. Read both passages carefully and then answer all the questions, before checking your answers with the model answers that follow.

Extract A *My Childhood*

Grandmother, sitting near me, was combing her hair and muttering something with a knitted brow. She had an extraordinary amount of hair which fell over her shoulders and breast to her knees, and even touched the floor. It was blue-black. Lifting it up from the floor with one hand and holding it with difficulty, she introduced an almost toothless wooden comb into its thick strands. Her lips were twisted, her dark eyes sparkled fiercely, while her face, encircled in that mass of hair, looked comically small. Her expression was almost malignant, but when I asked why she had such long hair she answered in her usual,

10   mellow, tender voice: 'Surely God gave it to me as a punishment . . . Even when it is combed, just look at it! When I was young I was proud of my mane, but now I am old I curse it. But you go to sleep. It is quite early. The sun has only just risen.'

'But I don't want to go to sleep again.'

'Very well, then don't go to sleep,' she agreed at once, plaiting her hair and glancing at the berth on which my mother lay rigid, with upturned face. 'How did you smash that bottle last evening? Tell me about it quietly.'

20   So she always talked, using such words that they took root in my memory like fragrant, bright, everlasting flowers. When she smiled the pupils of her dark, luscious eyes dilated and beamed with an inexpressible charm, and her strong white teeth gleamed cheerfully. Apart from her multitudinous wrinkles and her swarthy complexion, she had a youthful and brilliant appearance. What spoiled her was her bulbous nose, with its distended nostrils, and red lips, caused by her habit of taking pinches of snuff from her black snuff-box mounted with silver, and by her fondness for drink. Everything about her was dark,

30   but within she was luminous with an inextinguishable, joyful and ardent flame, which revealed itself in her eyes. Although she was bent, almost humpbacked, in fact, she moved lightly and softly, for all the world like a huge cat, and was just as gentle as that caressing animal.

Until she came into my life I seemed to have been asleep, and hidden away in obscurity; but when she appeared she woke me and led me into the light of day. Connecting all my impressions by a single thread, she wove them into a pattern of many colours, thus making herself my

40   friend for life, she being nearest my heart, the dearest and best known

of all; while her love for all creation enriched me, and built up the strength needful for a hard life.

Extract B *The Life and Loves of a She-Devil*

My mother was pretty enough, and ashamed of me. I could see it in her eyes. I was her eldest child. 'The image of your father,' she'd say. She'd married again, of course, by then. She'd left my father long ago, far behind, despised. My two half-sisters both took after her; they were delicate, fine-boned things. I liked them. They knew how to charm, and they charmed even me. 'Little ugly duckling,' my mother said to me, almost weeping, smoothing my wiry hair. 'What are we to do with you? What's to become of you?' I think perhaps she would have loved me, if she could. But ugly and discordant things revolted her: she couldn't help it. She said as much often enough: not of me, particular-   10 ly, of course, but I knew the patterns of her thought, I knew what she meant. I was born, I sometimes think, with nerve endings not inside but outside my skin: they shivered and twanged. I grew lumpish and brutish in the attempt to seal them over, not to know too much.

And I could never, you see, even for my mother's sake, learn just to smile and stay quiet. My mind struck keys like a piano dreadfully out of tune, randomly played, never quiet. She christened me Ruth, wanting, I think, even in my first days, to forget me if she could. A short, dismissive, sorrowful name. My little half-sisters were called Jocelyn   20 and Miranda. They married well, and disappeared, no doubt into contentment, bathed in the glow of the world's admiration.

SAMPLE QUESTIONS AND ANSWERS

1 Express in your own words what impression you get of the grandmother in the first paragraph only of Extract A.   (6)
2 The author uses figurative language in the paragraph beginning 'So she always talked . . .', to help him describe his grandmother. An example of this is: 'using such words that they took root in my memory like fragrant, bright, everlasting flowers'. Choose other examples of figurative language from this paragraph and the last paragraph of the passage and explain fully the meaning of the words used in a figurative sense.   (12)
3 Read the first sentence of the third paragraph again from 'Until she came – the light of day'. Explain in your own words what you think the author means.   (4)
4 Explain in your own words why Ruth's mother in Passage B seemed to be ashamed of her.   (6)
5 'I was born, I sometimes think, with nerve endings not inside but outside my skin: they shivered and twanged' (line 12). Express in your own words what you think is meant by these words.   (4)
6 According to the last paragraph, what did the narrator find it hard to do? (5)
7 Compare the feelings the grandmother inspired in the narrator of Passage A with the feelings the mother provoked in the narrator of Passage B.   (8)

Qu. 1 She mutters to herself which makes her seem rather ill-tempered. Her twisted lips and her fierce, sparkling eyes add to this impression of bad temper. She looked almost evil but her gentle voice when she answered her grandson softened this impression.

Qu. 2 *'she was luminous with an inextinguishable, joyful and ardent flame'*: Here the author wishes to express something about the energy or the power the grandmother has – 'flame' – which lights her up from the inside and spreads to those around her. This enthusiasm could not be dampened and she radiated joy.

'for all the world like a huge cat': Her movements were delicate and agile like a tiger or lion – full of strength but effortless.

'by a single thread, she wove them into a pattern of many colours': It is as if she knitted all the impressions the boy received together and made life full of colour and joy for him.

Qu. 3 This means that the grandmother gives the boy life; she breathes life into him, leading him out of uncertainty and insecurity to life and happiness. She opens life out for him.

Qu. 4 The mother seemed to be ashamed of her because she wasn't pretty like her two half-sisters and possibly because she was the product of her failed marriage with the girl's father whom she now disliked. Unlike her half-sisters, Ruth didn't know how to be charming and her mother did not like ugly or charmless things or people.

Qu. 5 She became so sensitive and anxious that it was almost as though her nerves were exposed on the surface of her skin rather than beneath it.

Qu. 6 She could never keep quiet just to please her mother. She was always saying and doing awkward things; she never seemed to strike the right note with her mother and fit in with her expectations.

Qu. 7 The boy felt the grandmother spread joy in his life, loved him and helped to understand and appreciate the world. In contrast the girl felt the mother did not love her; she felt rejected and she was filled with a sense of injustice. She resented her situation and felt unwanted.

Notes **1** asks you to interpret the material in the first paragraph about the grandmother. Use your own words as far as possible and select only relevant details. **2** asks you to pick out figurative language and explain fully the meaning of the figures of speech. **3** asks you to explain the meaning of a sentence. **4** asks you to extract information from the passage and express it in your own words as far as possible. **5** again asks for an explanation of meaning. **6** asks you to extract information. **7** gives you an opportunity to interpret material and write a comparison between the two passages.

You may be presented with contrasting newspaper accounts of the same events. You will be tested on your ability to detect the use of persuasive language, how reports can be slanted by the selection of some details and the exclusion of others, and your understanding of the general standpoint of a report.

Below are contrasting reports about events on one day of a miners' strike; they appeared in different newspapers. Read the reports carefully and then answer all the questions, before checking your answers with the model answers.

Report A

Pit police face petrol bombs in 7-hour fury

The National Coal Board's intensive campaign to persuade more miners to return in the heartland Yorkshire coalfields was answered yesterday with an unprecedented eruption of violence and civil disorder.

At the beginning of a critical week in the eight-month dispute the anger, frustration and pent-up emotion fuelled by the deadlocked strike boiled over in clearly co-ordinated attacks in pit villages across the area.

Petrol bombs were used against a police station and police vehicles for the first time in South Yorkshire; barricades burned through the early hours in many villages and shops were looted against a backdrop of the now-familiar confrontations between police, clad in riot equipment, and pickets hurling a barrage of stones and bottles.

By the end of the morning which saw trouble at more than half of Yorkshire's 53 collieries, 45 men had been arrested and 33 policemen injured, 12 requiring hospital treat-ment. At least nine pickets were also hurt in the clashes, which signified a change in tactics by the strikers.

But their attempt to stem the increased drift back to work in Yorkshire failed to prevent 614 men crossing the picket lines to clock on at 32 of the area's pits, 342 more than at the end of last week.

In a radio interview yesterday, Mr Arthur Scargill, the miners' president, again blamed the police as the cause of the violence. His comments drew a quick response from Mr Peter Wright, the Chief Constable of South Yorkshire, who had spent the morning collating reports of dozens of incidents in his office.

He later told a press conference at the Sheffield headquarters of South Yorkshire police: 'It is nonsense that we are to blame for everything that has gone on and it is repeated ad nauseam. I can only draw the conclusion that it is the policy of the NUM to blame the police.'

Report B
Police in brutal raid on strike centre

There were serious clashes at a number of pits in the Barnsley and South Yorkshire area yesterday.

At the Barrow pit, near Barnsley, 10 miners including the NUM branch secretary, Dave McDevitt, were arrested, while at the Dearne Valley colliery, where scabs were prevented from returning to work, six pickets were arrested.

In Rossington police kicked their way into the strike centre at the local miners' welfare, damaging property and injuring several miners.

At Sharlston police carrying shields used their truncheons against a crowd of 150 pickets when the scab wagon arrived carrying seven strike breakers. There were two arrests and two miners suffered injuries.

Later after three union officials were able to talk to them, the miners at Sharlston all came back out, leaving the pit scab-free.

Rossington NUM branch treasurer Peter Donnelly gave an account to the Star of the violence that erupted when police forced their way into the building.

'The police came charging in with full riot gear, carrying shields and truncheons drawn, chasing half a dozen lads who had just been leaving to go down to picket duty at the pit. They ran about indiscriminately beating and truncheoning our lads to the ground, kicking them. I shouted in protest and told them to get out. I was given a lot of abuse and was told to "shut my mouth".'

'A couple of officers had to restrain other policemen from the beating and kicking they were giving our NUM members.'

SAMPLE QUESTIONS AND ANSWERS
1 Compare the headlines used above the two reports. How do they reflect a contrast in emphasis between the two reports? (6)
2 In Report A, how is the reader given the impression that the violence stemmed from the miners? Quote evidence from the article using your own words as far as possible. Do not refer to the headline. (8)
3 In Report B, how is the reader given the impression in paragraphs 3–6 ('In Rossington . . . into the building') that the police were the aggressors? Again quote evidence from this part of the report, using your own words as far as possible. (8)
4 How do the two reports differ in the presentation of 'facts' about strikers returning to work? (8)
5 Who is directly quoted in Report A and who in Report B? What is the effect of having direct quotations by a spokesperson from only one side in a news report? (10)
6 What particular words or phrases are used in both the articles that might influence a reader's response to the reports? (12)

Qu. 1 The headline to Report A emphasises that the police on duty at the pits were the target of petrol bombs over a period of seven hours. The headline of Report B stresses that the police brutally raided a centre for striking miners. The first headline makes it appear the miners were responsible for the violence, the second that it was the police.

Qu. 2 The first and second paragraphs mention the outbreak of violence, unrest and organised attacks in mining villages. Then in the third paragraph this is followed up by the details of the petrol bombs thrown at a police station, looting and barricades. The pickets are described as hurling stones and bottles; the police are seen as the targets. The number of injured policemen is given as thirty-three, which far exceeds the nine pickets injured. The 'clashes' are reported as being a change of tactics on the miners' part, which suggests that they deliberately planned them.

Qu. 3 In Report B it is reported that the police kicked their way in to a strike centre, causing damage to property and injuries to miners. They are reported as having used their truncheons; no police injuries are reported but the injuries to two miners are.

Qu. 4 Report A states that 614 men had returned to work, which was an increased number. No figures for miners returning to work are quoted in Report B, except for the seven 'strike breakers' who were then, it is alleged in the report, persuaded to return to the strike.

Qu. 5 In Report A, a statement by Arthur Scargill is briefly referred to but the Chief Constable's statement is given greater space. His actual words denying Scargill's charges against the police are quoted. In Report B, the NUM branch treasurer's account of the police action is given in his own words, but there is no statement from the police. This gives added weight to the spokesman for the miners, as his version of the incident is not contradicted. In Report A the police spokesman's opinions are given much greater prominence, so it is this that makes an impression on the reader.

Qu. 6 In Report A 'unprecedented eruption of violence and civil disorder' gives the impression of a dreadful breakdown of law and order. 'Anger, frustration and pent-up emotion' suggest the miners are losing control and 'clearly co-ordinated attacks' implies that the violence is definitely organised. The words 'looted' and 'hurling a barrage' add to this impression.

In Report B, the use of the word 'scabs' shows that the writer disapproves of miners returning to work. The police 'kicked their way into' a miners' centre; that suggests they were deliberately starting trouble. Later they are described as 'indiscriminately beating and truncheoning our lads to the ground', which suggests brutal attacks on defenceless miners. When the miners' spokesman protested 'a lot of abuse' was hurled and some police even had to restrain their colleagues.

Extract: *Truth and Consequences*

Read the following short story and answer the questions that follow, before
checking your answers with the model answers and notes.

She had straight blond hair and a red mouth, and she was lame. Every
day she played golf and went swimming in the center of a crowd of
boys. Charles, sitting with his mother on the hotel porch, watched her
and nodded while his mother repeated, 'Isn't it extraordinary, a girl
like that? I wonder what in the world they see in her.' Charles took to
walking past the pool during the morning as the girl and boys lay there
side by side, laughing. He listened carefully to her voice. It was low,
unhurried, forceful. So, he thought, was her language. Every other
word seemed to him to be 'damn,' 'hell,' and worse. She spoke of God,
10 to whom Charles was preparing to dedicate his life, as if He were a
friend in the next block. 'I swear to God,' the girl said. 'I must have told
you this one, for God's sake.' Charles walked out of range of the jokes
that followed. He was eighteen and he was spending this last vacation
with his mother before entering a seminary. In eight more summers he
would be a priest. The girl's language sent sharp lightnings through
him. He had never seen or heard anyone like her before in his life.

One night after dinner, while his mother was upstairs swallowing a
pill, the girl sat down beside him on the hotel porch. Her lips were
smiling, her eyes the color of her blue, open blouse. 'We ought to know
20 each other,' she said. 'You ought to join the rest of us at the pool.'

'I'm with Mother.'

The girl covered his hand with hers. 'Well, for God's sake, you're
old enough to swim by yourself, aren't you?'

Charles felt that he ought to explain before it was too late, before she
had said something he could never forget. 'I'm going to be a priest,' he
said.

The girl kept smiling. 'A priest? With a turn-around collar and
everything?'

He nodded.

30 'So you can't come swimming with the gang?'

'That hasn't anything to do with it. I just thought I ought to tell you. I
always do tell people.'

'You can still come dancing with us if you want to?'

'Certainly.'

'Could you take me to a movie if you wanted to?'

'Yes.'

'I never met a boy who was going to be a priest. Could you take me
out for a ride tonight if you wanted to?'

He said in relief, 'We didn't bring our car.'

'Oh, hell, I mean in my car. I mean just for example. I didn't say I'd go with you.' She stared at him slowly from head to foot. 'It would be funny, with a boy who was going to be a priest.'

Fortunately, Charles thought, his mother would be coming downstairs at any moment now. She would make short shrift of the girl. 'You oughtn't to keep swearing like that,' he said.

He expected her to laugh, but she didn't. She ran her hand up and down the bare brown leg that was shorter than the other. 'Like what?' she said.

'Like "for God's sake." That's taking the name of the Lord in vain. That's one of the Ten Commandments.'

'I'm an awful damn fool,' the girl said. 'I talk like that to keep people from thinking about my leg. But I didn't know you were going to be a priest.'

Charles wanted to get rid of her, but he didn't know how. He stood up and said, 'I don't think you ought to worry about things like that. I hadn't even noticed.'

She stood up beside him. Her eyes shone in the mountain light. 'Oh, damn you, please don't lie to me,' she said. 'Of course you've noticed. But does it bother you? Does it make you want to stay away from me?'

'No,' he said. 'Oh, no.'

She slipped her hand under his arm. 'Thanks for saying that so nice and hard. I haven't asked anybody that in a long time.'

Without having willed it, stupidly, Charles found himself walking the length of the porch beside the girl. Her blond hair touched the shoulder of his coat. It was difficult to tell, looking down at her, that she was lame. He bent his head to smell her perfume. 'Tell me what you do,' he said.

'You mean, bang, just like that, what do I do?'

'Not that you have to tell me.'

'But I do. It's just that there aren't any surprises in me. I'm not beautiful or tormented – or not much tormented. I don't do anything. I got out of Walker's and I had a party and now I guess I'll be on the loose like this for a couple of years. Finally somebody may ask me to marry him, and quick like a fish I will. I hope I'll have sense enough for that. And I'll be terribly glad when I've done it. I'll try to let him win most of the arguments we'll have. I'll try to be good about satisfying him, the way all those awful books say, and about having good kids for him, and all that.'

Charles felt himself stumbling. She had told him everything about herself. She had told him the truth, which he hadn't wanted. They reached the end of the porch and stood facing the valley between the mountains. Two old men were playing croquet in the gathering darkness, the wooden mallets and balls knocking softly together, the white trousers moving like disembodied spirits across the lawn.

Charles and the girl could hear, below them in the kitchen, the clatter
of dishes being washed and stacked and the high, tired voices of the
waitresses.

'Now talk about you,' the girl said. 'You think you want to be a
priest?'

90   'Why – yes.'

'It isn't just a vow your mother made while she was carrying you?'

Charles laughed, and was surprised at how easily he laughed. 'Well,'
he said, 'I guess Mother's always wanted me to be a priest, especially
after Dad died. We went abroad then, Mother and I. We spent the
summer in Rome. We had an audience with the Pope – the old one, a
little man with thick glasses and a big ring. We got so we were going to
Mass and even to Communion every day. When we came back to this
country I started in at a Catholic school. I liked it. I graduated this
year. I'm going down to the seminary in the fall. I guess I'll like that,

100 too.'

'But isn't there more to it than that?' the girl said. 'I'm not a Catholic
– I'm not anything – but don't you have to have some kind of a call,
bells ringing, something like that?'

'You mean a vocation. Yes. Well, I guess I have a vocation all right.'

'But what is it? How can you be sure?'

Charles gripped the railing of the porch. He had never been able to
answer that question. He remembered kneeling beside his mother's
bed, month after month, year after year. 'Don't you feel it, darling?'
his mother had whispered. 'Don't you feel how wonderful it will be?

110 Don't you feel how God wants you?' Charles had told himself finally
that he was able to answer that question. The next day his mother,
dabbing her eyes, had said, 'Here's my boy, Father Duffy, I'm giving
him to you.' And Father Duffy had said, 'Ah, you're an example to
Irish mothers everywhere. Are you sure you want to come with us,
boy?' 'Yes, Father, I do,' Charles had said, watching his mother. He
had spoken an answer, written an answer, lived an answer, but he had
never believed it. He had been waiting to believe it. Now he heard
himself saying, for the first time, 'No, I can't be sure.'

The girl said, 'Then you're not going to be a priest. You mustn't be.

120 Why are you so damned afraid to face the truth?'

Charles saw his mother walking heavily along the porch. He studied
her as if she were a stranger. What an enormous old woman she was,
and how strong she was, and how she had driven him! He took the girl's
hand. It was cool and unmoving. He felt the porch floor trembling
under his mother's approach.

Brendan Gill

SAMPLE QUESTIONS AND ANSWERS

1. What is the meaning of Charles's mother's first comment about the girl and how does Charles react to it? (4)
2. How does Charles react to the girl's words and language when he overhears her talking to her friends? (4)
3. What clues are given in the story between lines 17 and 25 ('One night after dinner – he said') about how Charles feels when the girl sits down beside him and starts talking? (8)
4. Explain in your own words their exchange of conversation about the girl's lameness. (8)
5. Summarise in your own words what the girl says she is going to do in the future. (6)
6. (a) 'I'm going down to the seminary in the fall' (line 98). Explain the full meaning of this sentence. (4)
   (b) 'But don't you have to have some kind of a call, bells ringing, something like that?' (lines 101–2). Explain what the girl means by this question. (4)
7. Explain how the decision that Charles was to become a priest had been taken. (6)
8. Explain in your own words how the story ends and what is suggested is going to happen next. (8)
9. Why do you think the story is called 'Truth and Consequences'? (10)
10. What is your reaction to the girl as a character? Do you find her interesting and sympathetic or not? (10)

Qu. 1 His mother is surprised that the girl is the centre of attraction of a crowd of boys, because she is lame – which the mother clearly thinks would make her less appealing. Charles nods, appearing to agree with her but perhaps thinking something different.

Qu. 2 He thought that she used forceful words which reflected a strong personality. Her language shocked him and he did not like the way she talked about God. He did not want to hear the jokes she was sharing with her friends.

Qu. 3 He states in rather a defensive manner that he was with his mother and mentions that he was going to become a priest. Both these statements seem to be said to warn her off. He was able to make the excuse 'in relief' about the car and avoid offering to take her to a movie. He thinks to himself that his mother would soon be with him and she would be able to deal with the girl.

Qu. 4 The girl explains that she uses strong language to draw attention from her lame leg. Charles tries to reassure her that he hadn't noticed she was lame but she does not believe him and 'damns' him for telling a lie. She seeks reassurance that it does not really matter to him. His firm reply pleases her and she admits she hasn't asked that question of anyone for some time.

Qu. 5 When someone asks her to marry him she will accept. She will try to be a 'good wife' by making her husband feel superior to her, by looking after his needs and bearing him children.

Qu. 6 (*a*) He was going to attend the training college for priests in the autumn.   (*b*) She asks whether, before he made the decision to become a priest, he shouldn't have had some special sign, or something important happen to him to make up his mind.

Qu. 7 His mother had always wanted him to become a priest. As a child he had had his mother suggest to him that God wanted him to be a priest. He had finally been convinced by this and when Father Duffy had asked if he wanted to join the church as a priest, he had said 'yes'.

Qu. 8 The girl tells him he shouldn't become a priest if he isn't sure about it and asks him why he doesn't face up to the truth. Charles sees his mother coming towards him and realises how heavily she had influenced him to take the decison. He takes the girl's hand as though to help him face up to his mother and the suggestion is that he is going to face up to her and tell her he is not going to become a priest.

Qu. 9 The girl's frankness about her leg and her future, her way of facing up to the truth about herself, influences Charles to face up to some truths about himself – that he is not at all sure about wanting to become a priest. It is like the game 'truth and consequences' in which you have to tell the truth about something and then face up to the consequences. The consequences for Charles are that he has to face up to his real feelings and face up to his mother and stand on his own feet.

Qu. 10 I think the girl is a very strong personality; she attracts lots of admirers despite her lameness because of her vitality and honesty. I like the way she is honest about her own insecurity about her leg and also her friendly, frank manner. She is intelligent and is able to work out that Charles hadn't made the decision about his becoming a priest. She is willing to lend him her support in facing up to his mother. I find her sympathetic because of those qualities of honesty, frankness, intelligence and courage.

Notes: **1** calls for some *interpretation* of the story; you have to *deduce* from the text what the meaning is. **2** asks you to *extract information* from the story and express it *in your own words*. **3** demands that you search for the *relevant information* in a particular section of the story and then *interpret* that information. **4** involves you in *interpreting* a section of conversation and then summarising it in your own words. **5** again asks you to *summarise* a section but some *interpretation* is called for, such as pointing out her ambition to be a 'good wife' and what she means by that. **6** (*a*) and (*b*) ask you *to explain the meaning of sentences in this context*. **7** asks you to absorb information and then *interpret it in your own words*. **8** asks you to sum up the ending of the story and to show you understand what it *implies* by suggesting what is likely to happen next. **9** again tests your *understanding* of the story. **10** asks you for a *personal response* and there is no one correct answer to this. The answer above is given only as an example; you could take an opposite point of view as long as you *back up your opinion with evidence* from the story.

You may also be presented with an unseen poem in this kind of examination paper. Or for the coursework folder, you may have to answer questions on poetry. You will be tested on your ability to interpret the meaning and theme of the poem, i.e. to show what you think the poem is about. You will also be tested on your ability to understand how the poet uses language, sometimes figurative language. You may also be asked to write expressively on a theme arising from the poem.

Read the poem below and then answer the questions that follow before checking your answers with the sample answers below.

Poem: *Baking Day*
Thursday was baking day in our house.
The spicy smell of new baked bread would meet
My nostrils when I came home from school and there would be
Fresh buns for tea, but better still were the holidays.

Then I could stay and watch the baking of the bread.
My mother would build up the fire and pull out the damper
Until the flames were flaring under the oven; while it was heating
She would get out her earthenware bowl and baking boards

Into the crater of flour in the bowl she would pour sugar
10 And yeast in hot water; to make sure the yeast was fresh
I had often been sent to fetch it from the grocer that morning,
And it smelt of the earth after rain as it dissolved in the sweet water.

Then her small stubby hands would knead and pummel
The dough until they became two clowns in baggy pantaloons,
And the right one, whose three fingers and blue stump
Told of the accident which followed my birth, became whole.

As the hands worked a creamy elastic ball
Took shape and covered by a white cloth was set
On a wooden chair by the fire slowly to rise:
20 To me the most mysterious rite of all.

From time to time I would peep at the living dough
To make sure it was not creeping out of the bowl.
Sometimes I imagined it possessed, filling the whole room,
And we helpless, unable to control its power to grow,

But as it heaved above the rim of the bowl mother
Was there, taking it and moulding it into plaited loaves
And buns, and giving me a bit to make into a bread man,
With currant eyes, and I, too, was a baker.

My man was baked with the loaves and I would eat him for tea.
30 On Friday night when the plaited loaves were placed
Under a white napkin on the dining table,
Beside two lighted candles, they became holy.

No bread will ever be so full of the sun as the pieces
We were given to eat after prayers and the cutting of this bread.
My mother, who thought her life had been narrow, did not want
Her daughters to be bakers of bread. I think she was wise.

Yet sometimes when my cultivated brain chafes at kitchen
Tasks, I remember her, patiently kneading dough
And rolling pastry, her untutored intelligence
40 All bent towards nourishing her children.

Rosemary Joseph

SAMPLE QUESTIONS AND ANSWERS
Section A
1 Why did the poet think the holidays were better? (4)
2 The mother's hands would knead and pummel the dough 'until they became two clowns in baggy pantaloons.' Explain the meaning of this in full. (6)
3 How did the mother's hand 'become whole'? (4)
4 'To me the most mysterious rite of all' (line 20). What do you think the poet means by this? (6)
5 'My mother, who thought her life had been narrow, did not want her daughters to be bakers of bread. I think she was wise.' Explain in your own words what these two lines mean to you. (8)
6 (a) What do you think 'my cultivated brain' (line 37) means? (3)
   (b) What lasting image does the poet have of her mother, according to the last verse? (6)

Section B
Choose one of the following topics to write about, in prose, poetry or play-script. You should write between 200 and 250 words.
1 Describe a special day in your own or an imaginary household. This 'special' day is a regular occurrence in the household like baking day in the poem.
2 'A Working Day'

Section A
Qu. 1 She thought the holidays were better because during school term she only saw and enjoyed the product of her mother's baking but in the holidays she could actually watch her mother baking the bread and the buns.

Qu. 2 Her hands would be covered with the sticky dough so they appeared to have formed the shape of clowns with baggy pants. The dough clung to her hands and bulged outwards in places.

Qu. 3 Some accident had deprived the mother of one finger and taken off part of the thumb; the dough sticking to her hand covered up the gaps and made the hand seem to be complete again.

Qu. 4 She looks on the rising of the dough as a magic ritual, something miraculous that she cannot really understand.

Qu. 5 The impression is that the mother had spent her life looking after her family; baking for them was just one of the many tasks she carried out in catering for her children. She wanted something better for her daughters because she thought being a housewife and mother too limiting. The poet agrees with her mother's ambition for her children.

Qu. 6 (*a*) This means the poet has been educated; her mind has been broadened through education (*b*) Her image is of her mother's patience in carrying out her baking tasks which is in contrast with her own irritation with the household tasks. Her mother was not educated but she used her intelligence entirely in looking after and loving her children.

Notes on Section A **1** is a straightforward *information* question and correct answers depend on a careful reading of the poem. **2** asks you to *interpret the language and the meaning* of these lines. **3** again asks you to *interpret meaning*. **4** asks you to *interpret meaning* but it asks for more than just superficial information. You also have to *respond to* the line of poetry. **5** asks you to give your *personal response* to these lines. You must always be prepared to respond to expressive literature if you are required to. The examiners are interested in your opinions, your responses. **6**(*a*) asks you to explain a use of language in the poem; **6**(*b*) asks you for an interpretation of what is one of the themes of the poem.

Notes on Section B If this kind of assignment crops up in your course work, you will be judged largely on how you respond personally to the given poem. If you write a poem yourself in response to the material, then you may be able to submit it, and poems you write at other times in the course, to form one unit of writing for your folder, as long as you make it clear to the examiners what material it is (extract, poem, play, complete book) you are responding to.

You may also be faced with an extract from a play and be asked questions that test your understanding of the language, content and themes.

Read the following extract from a play and then answer the questions that follow before checking your answers with the model answers.

Extract: *Top Girls*

The scene is set in an employment agency, 'Top Girls'; this agency specialises in finding good jobs for well-qualified women. Nell is an employee of the agency; she is interviewing Shona to see if she is suitable for the post of a sales representative.

Interview

NELL *and* SHONA.

NELL: Is this right? You are Shona?

SHONA: Yeh.

NELL: It says here you're twenty-nine.

SHONA: Yeh.

NELL: Too many late nights, me. So you've been where you are for four years, Shona, you're earning six basic and three commission. So what's the problem?

SHONA: No problem.

NELL: Why do you want a change?

SHONA: Just a change.

NELL: Change of product, change of area?

SHONA: Both.

NELL: But you're happy on the road?

SHONA: I like driving.

NELL: You're not after management status?

SHONA: I would like management status.

NELL: You'd be interested in titular management status but not come off the road?

SHONA: I want to be on the road, yeh.

NELL: So how many calls have you been making a day?

SHONA: Six.

NELL: And what proportion of those are successful?

SHONA: Six.

NELL: That's hard to believe.

SHONA: Four.

NELL: You find it easy to get the initial interest do you?

SHONA: Oh yeh, I get plenty of initial interest.

NELL: And what about closing?

SHONA: I close, don't I?

NELL: Because that's what an employer is going to have doubts about with a lady as I needn't tell you, whether she's got the guts to push through to a closing situation. They think we're too nice. They think we listen to the buyer's doubts. They think we consider his needs and his feelings.

SHONA: I never consider people's feelings.

NELL: I was selling for six years, I can sell anything, I've sold in three continents, and I'm jolly as they come but I'm not very nice.

SHONA: I'm not very nice.

NELL: What sort of time do you have on the road with the other reps? Get on all right? Handle the chat?

SHONA: I get on. Keep myself to myself.

NELL: Fairly much of a loner are you?

SHONA: Sometimes.

NELL: So what field are you interested in?

SHONA: Computers.

NELL: That's a top field as you know and you'll be up against some very slick fellas there, there's some very pretty boys in computers, it's an American-style field.

SHONA: That's why I want to do it.

NELL: Video systems appeal? That's a high-flying situation.

SHONA: Video systems appeal OK.

NELL: Because Prestel have half a dozen vacancies I'm looking to fill at the moment. We're talking in the area of ten to fifteen thousand here and upwards.

SHONA: Sounds OK.

NELL: I've half a mind to go for it myself. But it's good money here if you've got the top clients. Could you fancy it do you think?

SHONA: Work here?

NELL: I'm not in a position to offer, there's nothing officially going just now, but we're always on the lookout. There's not that many of us. We could keep in touch.

SHONA: I like driving.

NELL: So the Prestel appeals?

SHONA: Yeh.

NELL: What about ties?

SHONA: No ties.

NELL: So relocation wouldn't be a problem.

SHONA: No problem.

NELL: So just fill me in a bit more could you about what you've been doing.

SHONA: What I've been doing. It's all down there.

NELL: The bare facts are down here but I've got to present you to an employer.

SHONA: I'm twenty-nine years old.

NELL: So it says here.

SHONA: We look young. Youngness runs in the family in our family.

NELL: So just describe your present job for me.

SHONA: My present job at present. I have a car. I have a Porsche. I go up the M1 a lot. Burn up the M1 a lot. Straight up the M1 in the fast lane to where the clients are, Staffordshire, Yorkshire, I do a lot in Yorkshire. I'm selling electric things. Like dishwashers, washing machines, stainless steel tub are a feature and the reliability of the programme. After sales service, we offer a very good after sales service, spare parts, plenty of spare parts. And fridges, I sell a lot of fridges specially in the summer. People want to buy fridges in the summer because of the heat melting the butter and you get fed up standing the milk in a basin of cold water with a cloth over, stands to reason people don't want to do that in this day and age. So I sell a lot of them. Big ones with big freezers. Big freezers. And I stay in hotels at night when I'm away from home. On my expense account. I stay in various hotels. They know me, the ones I go to. I check in, have a bath, have a shower. Then I go down to the bar, have a gin and tonic, have a chat. Then I go into the dining room and have dinner. I usually have fillet steak and mushrooms, I like mushrooms. I like smoked salmon very much. I like having a salad on the side. Green salad. I don't like tomatoes.

NELL: Christ, what a waste of time.

SHONA: Beg your pardon?

NELL: Not a word of this is true, is it?

SHONA: How do you mean?

NELL: You just filled in the form with a pack of lies.

SHONA: Not exactly.

NELL: How old are you?

SHONA: Twenty-nine.

NELL: Nineteen?

SHONA: Twenty-one.

NELL: And what jobs have you done? Have you done any?

SHONA: I could, though, I bet you.

SAMPLE QUESTIONS AND ANSWERS

1 'You're earning six basic and three commission. So what's the problem?' What does Nell mean by this?   (5)
2 'But you're happy on the road.' What does Nell mean by this?   (4)
3 'You'd be interested in titular management status but not come off the road?' Explain in full what Nell's question means here.   (4)
4 (a) What do you think Nell means by a 'closing' situation?   (4)
   (b) According to Nell, what doubts is an employer going to have about a 'lady' as a salesperson?   (5)
5 Why do you think Shona says 'I never consider people's feelings', and 'I'm not very nice.'?   (6)
6 'I'm as jolly as they come but I'm not very nice.' What does Nell mean by this?   (5)
7 Read Shona's long speech about her present job. What is there about the details she gives about her job that convinces Nell that she is telling a pack of lies?   (8)
8 'I could, though, I bet you.' What do you think Shona is admitting in this statement?   (4)
9 From your reading of this scene, what kind of characteristics would an actress playing (a) Nell and (b) Shona try to give them when playing them on stage?   (8)

Qu. 1   It means that Shona earns a basic salary of six thousand pounds a year and an additional three thousand in commission on the sales she makes, so why is she thinking of changing her job? The implication is that this is a good wage to be earning.

Qu. 2   Nell asks whether Shona is happy being a travelling saleswoman, moving from place to place by car.

Qu. 3   She asks whether Shona would like to be on a management level in name only while continuing to be a sales representative. Management usually involves an administrative job rather than selling things directly.

Qu. 4   (a)   Nell means the time when a salesperson moves to complete a sale; having interested the customer and almost made the sale, there is the psychological moment when a salesperson suggests completing the sale to the customer. (*b*) the employer thinks women don't have the courage to push for a sale; employers think women care too much about the customer's wishes and need to be more pushy.

Qu. 5 Shona is trying to impress Nell with her suitability for the job; she thinks Nell wants to be convinced that she is hard and ruthless, the qualities that seem to be associated with being a good salesperson.

Qu. 6 Nell appears to mean that she is good-humoured and pleasant on the surface, but quite cold and ruthless under the surface jolliness.

Qu. 7 A Porsche is an extremely expensive car and it seems unlikely that she would be given a car like that by her firm. She seems a bit vague about what she is selling – 'electric things'. Her reason for people wanting to buy fridges in the summer seem very silly, not the kind of reasons a salesman would give. She repeats herself a lot and doesn't really seem to know what to say. She gives irrelevant details about what she does at the hotels and even tells Nell what she usually has for dinner. She is talking nonsense and gives Nell no real idea of what she is supposed to be doing. She tells her about her favourite foods instead. It is obvious to Nell that she has never done the job.

Qu. 8 When Nell asks her whether she has ever had a job, she says she's sure she could do 'some', which suggests she hasn't done any at all; she is claiming she could if she were given the chance.

Qu. 9 An actress playing Nell would give her a business-like air; she might appear rather hard, but certainly intelligent and shrewd. She will seem very sure of herself but gives the appearance of acting out a role in life.

Shona will seem very anxious to please but very naive. She agrees readily with Nell, but when given the opportunity to talk at length about herself her total lack of experience should come through. Perhaps she might even be acted as though she is rather simple-minded, because many of the things she says are very immature, like a child.

Literary extracts
Read the extract below, and answer the questions that follow.

Extract: *Brighton Rock*

Hale knew, before he had been in Brighton three hours, that they meant to murder him. With his inky fingers and his bitten nails, his manner cynical and nervous, anybody could tell he didn't belong – belong to the early summer sun, the cool Whitsun wind off the sea, the holiday crowd. They came in by train from Victoria every five minutes, rocked down Queen's Road standing on the tops of the little local trams, stepped off in bewildered multitudes into fresh and glittering air: the new silver paint sparkled on the piers, the cream houses ran away into the west like a pale Victorian watercolour; a race in miniature motors, a band playing, flower gardens in
10 bloom below the front, an aeroplane advertising something for the health in pale vanishing clouds across the sky.

It had seemed quite easy to Hale to be lost in Brighton. Fifty thousand people besides himself were down for the day, and for quite a while he gave himself up to the good day, drinking gins and tonics wherever his programme allowed. For he had to stick closely to a programme: from ten to eleven Queen's Road and Castle Square, from eleven to twelve the Aquarium and Palace Pier, twelve till one the front between the Old Ship and West Pier, back for lunch between one and two in any restaurant he chose round the Castle Square, and after that he had to make his way all
20 down the parade to the East Pier and then to the station by the Hove streets. These were the limits of his absurd and widely advertised sentry-go.

Advertised on every 'Messenger' poster: 'Kolley Kibber in Brighton today'. In his pocket he had a packet of cards to distribute in hidden places along his route; those who found them would receive ten shillings from the 'Messenger', but the big prize was reserved for whoever challenged Hale in the proper form of words and with a copy of the 'Messenger' in his hand: 'You are Mr Kolley Kibber. I claim the *Daily Messenger* prize.'

This was Hale's job to do sentry-go, until a challenger released him, in every seaside town in turn: yesterday Southend, today Brighton,
30 tomorrow –

He drank his gin and tonic hastily as a clock struck eleven and moved out of Castle Square. Kolley Kibber always played fair, always wore the same kind of hat as in the photograph the 'Messenger' printed, was always on time. Yesterday in Southend he had been unchallenged: the paper liked to save its guineas occasionally, but not too often. It was his duty today to be spotted – and it was his inclination too. There were reasons why he didn't feel too safe in Brighton, even in a Whitsun crowd.

He leant against the rail near the Palace Pier and showed his face to the crowd as it uncoiled endlessly past him, like a twisted piece of wire, two by

two, each with an air of sober and determined gaiety. They had stood all the 40
way from Victoria in crowded carriages, they would have to wait in queues
for lunch, at midnight half asleep they would rock back in trains to the
cramped streets and the closed pubs and the weary walk home. With
immense labour and immense patience they extricated from the long day
the grain of pleasure: this sun, this music, the rattle of the miniature cars,
the ghost train diving between the grinning skeletons under the Aquarium
promenade, the sticks of Brighton rock, the paper sailors' caps.

Nobody paid attention to Hale; no one seemed to be carrying a 'Messenger'. He deposited one of his cards carefully on top of a little basket and
moved on, with his bitten nails and his inky fingers, alone. He only felt his 50
loneliness after his third gin; until then he despised the crowd, but afterwards he felt his kinship. He had come out of the same streets, but he was
condemned by his higher pay to pretend to want other things, and all the
time the piers, the peepshows pulled at his heart. He wanted to get back –
but all he could do was to carry his sneer along the front, the badge of
loneliness. Somewhere out of sight a woman was singing. 'When I came up
from Brighton by the train': a rich Guinness voice, a voice from a public
bar. Hale turned into a private saloon and watched her big blown charms
across the two bars and through a glass partition.

She wasn't old, somewhere in the late thirties or the early forties and she 60
was only a little drunk in a friendly accommodating way. You thought of
sucking babies when you looked at her, but if she'd borne them she hadn't
let them pull her down: she took care of herself.

SAMPLE QUESTIONS
1 This extract is the opening section of a novel 'Brighton Rock'. If you were a
person picking up the book in a shop or a library, would you be 'grabbed'
by the opening sentence of the extract? Give reasons for your answer. (6)
2 What does the author mean by saying Hale 'didn't belong' (line 3)? (4)
3 How does the author manage to give a quick impression of Brighton in the
first paragraph? (6)
4 Explain briefly what Hale meant by his 'programme' (line 15)? (4)
5 Who was Kolly Kibber and what was he doing in Brighton? (4)
6 Why did Hale drink his gin-and-tonic hastily? (4)
7 What was Kolly Kibber's instructions for that day in Brighton? (4)
8 'With an air of sober and determined gaiety.' (line 40) What does this
phrase and the rest of the paragraph tell us about the crowd's attitude to
their day out? (6)
9 Why do you think Hale 'deposited one of his cards carefully on top of a
little basket' (line 49)? (4)
10 What effect did gin have on Hale? (4)
11 What had 'higher pay' (line 54) done to Hale? (4)
12 Explain the meaning of the phrase 'the badge of loneliness' (lines
55–6). (4)
13 Explain in your own words why Hale is attracted to the woman in the
public bar. (6)

Read the extract below, and answer the questions that follow.

Extract: *The Four-Gated City*
In front of Martha was grimed glass, its lower part covered with grimed muslin. The open door showed an oblong of browny-grey air swimming with globules of wet. The shop fronts opposite were no particular colour. The lettering on the shops, once black, brown, gold, white, was now shades of dull brown. The lettering on the upper part of the glass of this room said 'Joe's Fish and Chips' in reverse, and was flaking like stale chocolate.

She sat by a rectangle of pinkish oilcloth where sugar had spilled, and on to it, orange tea, making a gritty smear in which someone had doodled part of a name: Daisy Flet . . . Her cup was thick whitey-grey, cracked. The
10 teaspoon was a whitish plastic, so much used that the elastic brittleness natural to it had gone into an erosion of hair lines, so that it was like a kind of sponge. When she had drunk half the tea, a smear of grease appeared half-way down the inside of the cup: a thumb mark. How hard had some hand – attached to Iris, to Jimmy? – gripped the cup to leave a smear which even after immersion in strong orange tea was a thumbprint good enough for the police?

Across the room, by another pinkish rectangle, sat Joe's mother Iris, a small, fattish smeared woman. She was half asleep, catnapping. She wore an overall washed so often it had gone a greyish yellow. A tired soured
20 smell came from her. The small fattish pale man behind the counter where the tea-urn dominated was not Joe, who had gone off to the war and had never returned home, having married a woman and her café in Birmingham. He was Jimmy, Joe's mother's partner. Jimmy wished to marry Iris, but she did not want to marry again. Once was enough she said. Meanwhile they lived together and proposed to continue to live together.

Although both were now 'resting', this being a slack time in the café, and had announced, as if they turning a notice on a door to say 'Closed', that they were resting, both observed Martha. Or, rather, their interest, what was alert of it, was focused on what she would do next, but they were too
30 good-mannered to let this appear. About an hour before she had asked if she might use the telephone. She had not yet done so. From time to time the two exchanged remarks with each other, as thickly indifferent as words coming out of sleep, sleep-mutters; but yet it was open to Martha to join in if she wished, to comment on the weather and the state of Jimmy's health, neither very good. Today he had a pain in his stomach. Really they wanted to be told, or to find out, why the telephone call was so important that Martha could not make it and be done. The air of the small steamy box which was the café vibrated with interest, tact, curiosity, sympathy – friendship, in short; all the pressures which for a blissful few weeks since
40 Martha had been in England, rather, London, she had been freed from.

For a few weeks she had been anonymous, unnoticed – free. Never before in her life had she known this freedom. Living in a small town anywhere means preserving one's self behind a mask. Coming to a big city for those who have never known one means first of all, before anything else, and the more surprising if one has not expected it, that freedom: all the pressures are off, no one cares, no need for that mask. For weeks, then, without boundaries, without definition, like a balloon drifting and bobbing, nothing had been expected of her.

SAMPLE QUESTIONS
1 Why do you think the author has deliberately repeated the word 'grimed' in the first sentence of the extract? (4)
2 Read the first paragraph of the extract again. What kind of impression of the place she is describing is the author trying to give the reader? (6)
3 What details does the writer use in the second paragraph only of the extract to give the impression of dirty surroundings? (6)
4 'Across the room, by another pinkish rectangle' (line 17). What is meant by 'pinkish rectangle' here? (4)
5 What was Iris's attitude to marriage? (6)
6 Explain in your own words the full meaning of the first sentence of the fourth paragraph (lines 26–28). (4)
7 Why was Martha the focus of Iris's and Jimmy's interest at that moment? (4)
8 What was the manner, and the main subjects, of the conversation Iris and Jimmy exchanged? (4)
9 What things are involved in friendship, according to the last paragraph? (4)
10 Why had the few weeks she had spent in England been 'blissful' for Martha? (4)
11 'For a few weeks she had been anonymous' (line 41). Explain the meaning of 'anonymous' in this sentence. (4)
12 What does the last paragraph have to say about living in a small town? (4)
13 According to the last paragraph, how is the big city different from life in a small town? (4)
14 Express in your own words what kind of picture of the café, the people and their relationships the author has created in this extract. (8)

Newspaper reports
Read these two passages about different aspects of the pop music industry, then answer the questions that follow.

Passage **A**
PEACE has returned to Europe. Silence fell at 5am when an Irishman blew a trumpet in his hotel bedroom and passed out. The Eurovision song contest was over for another year.

Many of you saw the final conflagration on your television screens last night, but there is no point dwelling on that. As President Reagan said, now is a time to forget past atrocities. However, there are things you should all know.

For a start, the Swedes have the highest suicide rate in the world and holding the Eurovision Song Contest in Gothenburg is not likely to help. There have been amazing scenes.

By Monday three plagiarism rows

had broken out. Sweden accused the British songwriters of stealing one of its hits, while the Brits accused the Italians, and the Israelis attacked the French on the same grounds. With a competition where all the songs are indistinguishable, even to those with years of musical training, this is hardly surprising.

Reporting this event is like covering the Falklands war. Journalists are "members of the British delegation" and answerable to its leader, James Moir, head of BBC Variety. We become part of the military machine and critical reports were not expected.

For example, a story could easily have been written headlined "Vikki Goes Bonkers in Euro Cock-up". Our girl, Vikki Watson, seemed to be going off her rocker all week and was neurotically terrified of losing her voice. While other singers went to parties on the hour, pinching each others' bottoms and so forth, Vikki stayed in her hotel room Taking It Seriously and inhaling steam from a kettle to counteract the dry Gothenburg air.

Passage B

THE RELEASE of the first album from Frankie Goes to Hollywood last week sees the culmination of a process which has created this year's biggest pop industry sensation.

Whether or not the advance orders of well over a million copies represent the biggest in pop history, as is being claimed, there's no doubt that Frankie are currently riding a tide of success extraordinary even by pop's jaded standards. Despite strong competition from heavyweights such as Wham!, Duran Duran and Culture Club, "Welcome To The Pleasure Dome" is bound to be the record stuffed into most stockings this Christmas.

Frankie Goes to Hollywood were a gamble that paid off, beyond their wildest dreams. It is to their credit that they have seized the power which it has given them and made their pleasure dome a place to dream. The album's attraction – apart from its plain cheek – is that it lives up to the references in the title, creating a lush, fervid environment which stimulates the imagination.

Yet in its completeness and the completeness of Frankie's success, lies the seeds of decline – a decline already anticipated on the inner sleeve as a group member states: "but if it all ends tomorrow, we've had a good ride, we've seen what it's like."

The people who queued up on Monday morning to buy "Welcome to the Pleasure Dome" were participating, as they were fully aware, in an event. In buying Frankie they were buying the idea of success as much as what the group have to offer.

Yet this begs a question: what happens when Frankie aren't successful? Where do they go from here? The record ends with an orchestral theme which states: "Frankie Say ... No More!", a strong hint that they would prefer to disappear rather than suffer anti-climax.

SAMPLE QUESTIONS

1 In the first two paragraphs of Passage A, how does the writer suggest that the Eurovision Song Contest was like a war? (8)

2 In the third paragraph how does the writer show that he does not think very highly of the contest? (4)

3 'Three plagiarism rows had broken out.' Read the whole of the 4th paragraph again, then explain what 'plagiarism' means. (5)

4 What, according to the writer, was expected of the British journalists? (4)

5 Why do you think the words 'Taking It Seriously' (last paragraph, Passage A) have capital letters? (4)

6 In paragraph one of Passage B which words tell us that the year's biggest pop industry sensation had been carefully planned? (4)

7 How many copies of the record had been ordered before the release? (2)

8 Which word is used in the second paragraph to suggest that the pop music industry is tired or lifeless? (2)

9 Explain in your own words what the writer says about the album in the third paragraph of Passage B. (6)

10 'Lies the seeds of decline.' What does the 4th paragraph suggest lies ahead for the group and how does one group member react to that? (6)

11 'In buying Frankie they were buying the idea of success as much as what the group have to offer.' What do you think this sentence means? (6)

12 Compare the tone used by the writers in A and B. In what way is their approach to writing about pop music different? (10)

Units of work

The examining board will make it clear in the English syllabus how many units of work candidates must submit in particular categories of course work. The syllabus will state something like this:

'Candidates must submit six units of work. Each unit should normally be about 500 words in length. While a unit may be a number of pieces of work related to one another, at least one of the units must be a single, continuous piece of writing.'

The first two sentences of that paragraph require little explanation; the number of units of work required and the normal length expected are clearly defined. The point about a unit possibly being a number of related pieces of work may need some further explanation, however.

Suppose you have written a number of shorter pieces round a theme, e.g. 'the city' or 'loneliness'. Some of these pieces might be quite short poems, for example, or short descriptive pieces. They will be far too short to submit as individual units of work, but they could be put together into one unit of work centred round the theme. Make sure you make this clear to the examiner in the coursework folder that this is intended as one unit of work. You could even make a separate cover for this unit and give it a bold title.

Always look for ways of presenting your course work in the best light. If the recommended length of each unit is between 400 and 500 words, never submit any one unit that is less than that length. If there is a way of submitting several shorter pieces as one unit, then do so.

When do you do the course work?

You can do most course work partly in the classroom, partly at home or all in the classroom or all at home. But certain syllabuses lay down that a certain proportion of the course work must be done *under controlled conditions*. The section in the syllabus relating to this will read like this:

'Two units out of the seven must be written under classroom super-vision, each session lasting for about an hour. One of these units should show discussion, argumentative or factual writing, one to show personal writing, and the other narrative or descriptive writing.'

You must see this writing, done under classroom supervision, as more or less like an examination. You must certainly take it as seriously as a public examination, because that is really what it is. The techniques we have advised you to use in the examination room in the other chapters of this book are absolutely relevant to these timed pieces of writing. Prepare yourself for them. Take them very seriously.

All your own work

All the writing you produce for your course work must be your own work. As we have already said, it is clear that course work written at a leisurely pace after drafting and redrafting, and advice from your teacher, will probably be better in some respects than most writing done in a public examination or even under supervised conditions. Examiners expect this. What you cannot do is copy any work at all, or get someone else to do part of the writing. If you do this, it will be obvious to the examiners. That is partly why there are units of course work that have to be done under classroom supervision. It is in a sense a check on the rest of the course work – that it is all your own work.

Drafting and redrafting

You are allowed, however, to do a first draft of writing produced for coursework assessment. In fact, we strongly advise you to do so.

After the initial planning stages, which we have advised you about elsewhere in this book, write a first draft of your piece and show this to your teacher, making clear that it is a first attempt. The teacher will advise you about how it could be improved. Then write the final version and submit it for assessment. This has to be the final version of your piece. You cannot receive the writing back from the teacher with all the corrections and comments added and then do another 'fair copy'. You have to stand by your final version you submitted for assessment.

Making a choice

You do not need to submit all the work you have produced during the course for the final coursework assessment. You should be in the position of selecting your *best pieces within the categories* laid down by the syllabus. The syllabus may state:

'The units of work submitted for assessment should consist of a selection of the candidate's best work produced during the course.'

The selection of the final submitted course work is a vital part of the process. Accept advice from your teacher. Make sure that, if you have to submit a certain number of units of certain kinds of writing (e.g. narrative, argumentative, factual), you meet exactly the demands of the examiners.

Choose the pieces you think show you at your best. Make sure each piece of work is dated. Some examining boards may insist each unit has some indication of the conditions under which it was produced (e.g. homework, classwork), either written on the work itself or on the contents page which should certainly precede the actual units of work:

1   The Lost Weekend: Narrative – homework.
2   Letters to firms about jobs: directed writing – classwork/homework.

More about course work

There are two main types of written course work required for GCSE English:

1 Expression or Continuous writing.
2 Understanding and Expression (including response to reading done during the course).

Expression

You will have to submit examples of writing in various modes or forms (see Chapter 2). The syllabus will probably state something like this:

'Candidates should submit six units of work to demonstrate a range of kinds of writing.'

You may think the strength of your writing lies in narrative or description or play-writing. It may well do, but the examiners have to have evidence of your ability to write in various modes. A folder of course work that consists almost completely of short stories, with little or no *range* of writing, will be penalised where it is stated clearly that a range of writing must be submitted. Always obey the *letter*, as well as the *spirit*, of the law as far as the syllabus is concerned.

Writing done under classroom supervision

Most examining boards demand that some – perhaps two or three – of the writing units submitted as course work must be done under classroom supervision. It is very likely that you will be given more than two or three opportunities to write under these conditions. The examining board will probably recommend this in the syllabus so that candidates produce a reasonable number of pieces from which to select the required number of units.

Although examination conditions cannot be applied in these timed writing sessions, you are entitled to expect quiet and freedom from interruption.

Remember, the examiners must be confident that writing produced under close classroom supervision is your best unrevised work. To produce this, you require your deepest concentration and the most favourable classroom atmosphere possible.

Understanding and Expression

This type of course work is designed to test candidates' response to reading. Although there is a separate English Literature examination, English at GCSE is seen as a unified subject, i.e. no real difference is made between English Language and English Literature.

Although no set books are listed for candidates to read, you are expected to have read for the English exam a wide range of literature as well as non-literary texts.

Response to reading

One of the units of work you could submit (it may be compulsory) is writing responding to the reading you have done during the GCSE course.

What examiners do *not* want are summaries or paraphrases of the content of a book without any personal response on your part. If all you do is read a book and then tell the examiner the story, you are achieving very little. The examiners want much more from you than that.

Examiners like you to give a *personal* response and express your own opinions about the reading you have done. Remember this, however: always back up your opinion by referring to sections of the book, poem or play. Avoid silly, sweeping generalisations that really tell the examiner nothing about your response:

> 'I thought it was boring.' or 'I thought it was the best book I have ever read.'

Both these statements might be true but it doesn't get you, or the examiner, very far. You must back up your opinions with good reasons reinforced by evidence from the books.

You can study several books by the same author, showing perhaps how similar themes crop up in several books. Or you could compare how different authors have dealt with the same theme in their books, short stories, poems or plays.

You can also respond to literature by entering 'into the skin' of one of the characters and writing something in character that is related to the story or play. For example, if you were studying *Romeo and Juliet* you might write extracts from Romeo's or Juliet's diary in which they comment in their own words on their feelings. Or you could write a report of the street battle between the Montagus and the Capulets as reported on the front page of the local Verona newspaper. There are all kinds of imaginative responses to the literature you read that allow you to write creatively and at the same time show you understand the story, themes and characters of the original.

Response to non-literary material

You could develop the approach we have asked you to take in several of the assignments set in the 'Understanding' chapter. You could compare two contrasting accounts of the same event or two expressions of opinion on a controversial social issue. You could analyse how language is used in advertising, or report on the results of some kind of opinion poll.

Oral course work and oral test

It depends on which examining board you are entered with as to how you are assessed in oral communication. It may be that you will be assessed only by course work, i.e. in various oral activities during the course and without having to take a final oral test. It may be that your final assessment in oral communication will be a combination of marks awarded for oral course work *and* marks awarded in an oral test near the end of the course.

In a sense, whether you are assessed by a combination of course work and oral test, by course work or oral test alone, your task is the same: to convince those who are assessing you that you can communicate effectively in various speech contexts:

> in a one-to-one situation, e.g. in a conversation with one other person or in an interview situation
> giving a prepared talk to a group
> playing a role in a given situation (role-playing, e.g. taking on the role of an interviewee at a job interview).

Just as you can improve your performance in written English by deliberately and systematically working on your weaknesses, so in oral work skills can be learned that will improve your performance and your assessment in oral communication. Do not take Oral Communication lightly.

You must achieve at least a grade 5 in this part of the English examination if you are to be awarded an overall grade in English. Grade 5, however, should be your minimum goal. In the future people will be looking at your GCSE English award and clearly a grade 1 or 2 in Oral Communication will impress them far more than a lower grade. If you are partly or wholly assessed by oral course work, take it very seriously.

How you are assessed

For a candidate to be awarded a grade 1 in Oral Communication, he or she would be expected to have shown competence in some or all of the following abilities:

> to understand and communicate quite complex information;
> to organise and present opinions, ideas and facts in an oderly and persuasive manner;
> to choose and evaluate relevant information from given material for particular purposes;
> to talk effectively about personal experience;
> to respond to other people's opinions and to be able to recognise particular arguments and opinions;
> to speak in an appropriate tone in various contrasting speech situations;
> to speak clearly, audibly and using appropriate language.

At the other end of the scale of awards, a grade 5 candidate would be expected to show competence in some or all of these abilities:

   to understand and communicate simple information, e.g. simple instructions;

   to present ideas, opinions and facts with a limited degree of clarity and range of expression;

   to pick out some details from given material for a fairly limited and straightforward purpose;

   to talk about personal experience clearly;

   to distinguish between statements of fact and statements of opinion;

   to show some awareness of the need to use different speech styles when speaking to different audiences;

   to speak clearly and audibly.

You will see from these outlines of what is expected for those two grade awards the different expectations of the examiners. It may not prove too difficult to gain a grade 5 award, provided you take part in the oral activities of the course and that you take the oral test if there is one, but you should not be at all satisfied with a minumum 'pass'.

Other kinds of preparation
There are activities you can join in outside the classroom which will help you improve your communication skills. For example, you could join in drama activities. You could also take part in debates in your school or college. Discussing matters with other students on a school or college council will also help you develop listening and responding skills.

   All these activities can be very important in building up your confidence in oral communication.

Nerves
You may think of yourself as a 'shy' or 'nervous' person who finds it difficult to join in on group discussions or to give a talk to a group. The fact is that *everyone* is nervous in certain situations. But being nervous does not need to be a handicap. You can make those nerves work for you.

   When you hear sports stars talk about their 'nerves' before a big occasion, they usually say they are glad to feel tense and nervous. If they did not feel that way, they would not feel they were 'tuned up' for the occasion. Nerves are a form of energy. You have to use that energy in a controlled way.

   Teachers and examiners are used to dealing with nervous candidates and they are sympathetic. They will assess you on how you control and use that nervousness.

Oral course work
For oral course work, you, the candidate, will be assessed on your ability in a wide range of speech situations. These can be fairly formal or informal

discussions; they could be stimulated by written texts, visual material, television or tape, or a prepared talk given by one of your group. You might also be asked to take part in a role-playing exercise or to improvise in drama.

Oral course work will involve continuous assessment and you will be judged on how well you have demonstrated relevant speech and listening skills over the duration of the course. A record of marks for your performance in oral work will be kept by your teacher and a final, all-over assessment based on this record of marks will be submitted to the examining board.

Your school or college will set up oral activities in pairs or groups during your course.

The ability to listen and respond

An important part of oral skills is the ability to listen to what other people are saying, whether it be in the form of opinions, ideas, information, accounts of personal experience or demonstrations. Your ability in oral communication will be judged partly on your skills in understanding and responding in an intelligent and sensitive manner to what other people are saying. This is testing the same kind of skills as are tested in Understanding and Response in written course work, but this time in an oral context.

Group discussion

Normally, group discussion will be organised in groups of four or five. The starting-point for group discussion may be something you are given to read (a newspaper article, a poem, some interesting statistics) or something you have seen (video tape, a film).

Clearly, group discussion will test your communication skills, but it will also test your social skills as well, e.g. your sensitivity towards other people and your interaction with them.

Consider this example:

> A group discussion is taking place and one member of the group is very dominant. This individual speaks far more often than the other people in the group and does not seem to want to listen to other people's contributions. He or she appears to be uninterested in the give-and-take of discussion and seems more interested in dominating the group.

Without doubt, this particular candidate would lose marks for being insensitive to the other members of the group. Remember, communication means *two-way* communication, i.e. people *exchanging* ideas, opinions, information. If this exchange does not take place, effective communication is absent; and if you are the person largely responsible for this lack of exchange, then you will certainly lose marks because of it.

Your aim in group discussion should not simply be to speak more than

anyone else in the group. You should take an equal part in the discussion.
Consider this further example:

> A member of a discussion group says very little during the discussion,
> perhaps only to the extent of a few words here and there. Even when
> another member of the group prompts this 'silent' individual, he or she
> fails to take an adequate share in the discussion.

This is the opposite danger to being over-dominant in group discussion:
saying far too little. You must learn to assert yourself in group discussion
without being too dominant, too 'bossy' or too shrill. You can be too good a
listener. Listening attentively is indeed one skill you must have, but you
should be able to absorb what you hear and express your responses.

The technique and skills involved in taking part in group discussions must
be learnt by you during the English course.

Role-playing exercises

Role-playing exercises involve you in playing a role in simulations of
real-life situations. Playing a role means you have to act as you think the
person whose role you are playing would in that particular real-life
situation (e.g. playing the role of a nervous job applicant at an interview,
playing the role of an employer at an interview, playing the role of a witness
to a minor crime or an accident).

The difference between role-playing and taking part in a dramatic
improvisation is not always very wide, but the main interest of your
teachers in assessing your contribution to a role play will be in how well you
have demonstrated your understanding of the role you have taken on, how
effectively you have interacted with the others in the group and how
intelligently you have adapted your speech to the particular role and
situation you find yourself in. Your appreciation of how *appropriate* various
kinds of speech are to differing situations will play an important part in the
assessment.

Giving a prepared talk

For oral course work or in an oral test you may be asked to give a prepared
talk on a subject of your own choice. Preparing a talk of two, three or four
minutes' duration needs careful thought and planning.

Preparation

If you have to give a prepared talk, or make some introductory remarks
before entering into a conversation with an examiner, then you must
prepare what you are going to say.

> Your talk must have a shape, a structure, a direction.
> You must not write your talk out word for word and then just read it.

You are not allowed to do this – it is a talk you are giving, not a reading. The other thing to avoid is learning your talk by heart and then delivering it 'parrot-style'.

You must prepare brief notes, writing them on a card. Refer to them during the talk, but do not depend too much on them.

What should your talk be about?

Normally you will be allowed to talk about any subject that interests you. You could give a talk about a hobby, a special interest you have, describe a skill you possess, demonstrate how something works or talk about something interesting that has happened to you or that you have been involved with. You could also give a talk about a social issue that you have strong opinions about.

It is essential you discuss the topic you are going to talk about with your teacher or at least with an adult whose judgement you can trust.

Planning

Once you have chosen your topic, start planning your talk.

A talk has to be signposted for the listener(s). Always try and put yourself in the position of the listener.

A talk must have:

A *beginning*: the introduction in which you inform your audience what your subject is and how you are going to deal with it in your talk.

A *middle*: the development in which the main body of your talk takes place. You may divide it into sections, as long as you make plain the different aspects of the subject you are dealing with in each section to your listener(s).

A *conclusion*: this should consist of either a brief *summary* of the main points of the talk or a *number of recommendations* you would like to make concerning the topic. Never just tail off limply. Always have a definite ending so that the listeners are in no doubt that the talk has ended.

Preparing a talk requires similar preparatory skills to writing a piece of written work.

You have to give clear signposts to your listeners, just as you have to with readers of your written work.

You have to have 'a sense of audience'. You must suit the content, tone and language of your talk to the audience who are listening.

You must use notes to help you plan what you are going to say, just as you use a skeleton outline to help you write a piece of continuous writing.

Making notes

It is best to use a postcard for your notes. Keep the notes very brief. You do not have to write complete sentences; brief phrases and/or key words will do. Use headings to remind you of the main points of the talk. A card of notes on the topic 'My summer holiday' might look like this:

Introduction

Booked package holiday Las Palmas; with parents; fortnight in the sun; my account of the 'ups and downs'.

Development

First time flying; first time abroad; nervous but controlled nerves after take-off.

First few days: sunburnt – too much sunbathing; tried local foods – enjoyed; beach, trips to interesting sights; disco in evening. Made new friends.

Leaving: very sad; exchanged addresses; flight home; presents, duty free; pouring on arrival.

Conclusion

Would go back; learnt from experience – strange customs, different ways. Hope to go abroad every year from now on.

There are enough notes on this card to signpost the direction of your talk. They are not too long and you would be able to expand on them by adding more details as you talked.

Delivery of a talk

Your first duty is to make sure your speech is clear and audible. You must also avoid a monotonous delivery by varying the pitch, tone and emphasis. If you say everything in the same way, with an equal stress on every word, in the same manner and not varying the pitch of your voice, you will lose the attention of your listeners, however good the content of your talk may be.

Timing

Part of planning a talk is timing how long it is going to take. To take much more time for your talk than is allowed is just as bad as running out of something to say well before the recommended length. You must time yourself giving the talk before the test. If it is too short in a practice run, then you must add something. If it is too long, you must cut out something.

Eye contact

Do not hold your head so that your eyes are facing downwards all the time. Allow yourself to have eye contact with the person or persons you are talking to, or they will feel left out of it.

Exercise

1 Plan a talk of about three minutes on any one of the following topics, using brief notes:

> an interest or hobby that you have
> your hopes for the future
> looking back on your schooldays
> a social issue you care about
> describing some special occasion or event you have been
>   involved in
> explaining how your area could be improved

2 Having planned your talk and completed your notes, practise it, if possible in front of other people (one person will do). Again, if possible, record it on a cassette tape and learn from the playback. Time the practice talk and make alterations according to whether it is too long or too short.

3 Now give your talk again with the improvements you have decided on. Again record it or find an audience of at least one person to give you advice about it.

Conversation

If, as part of an oral test or oral course work, you have to be assessed on your ability to carry on a conversation with an adult (a teacher or examiner), you should remind yourself that it *is* a conversation and not a question-and-answers session. It is not meant to take the form of the teacher or examiner throwing questions at you and your trying to find the right answers.

Think about the conversations you have in real life. They are an interchange between people, an *exchange* of conversation. In a conversation with an examiner or teacher you will be expected to do most of the talking.

Formal?

There is no escaping the fact that an oral test is a fairly formal occasion. The examiner will do his or her best to put you at your ease, however.

He or she will be testing your ability to communicate in conversation in these rather artificial circumstances. To do yourself full justice you must put aside any doubts you may have about the point of the whole exercise. You must take it very seriously, but at the same time try to be natural and forthcoming in your manner.

A sense of the occasion

Remember how we have stressed the need for you to adapt your speech (and your writing) to different situations and purposes. In a conversation with an examiner or a teacher you cannot really chat in the same way as you would with your friends. You may not know the examiner and yet you must get on a wavelength of communication with him or her.

What you will be tested on

Your abilities in the following will be tested:

> effective communication with an adult,
> listening and responding,
> carrying the conversation forward,
> using appropriate speech for the occasion,
> speaking clearly and audibly.

Because the conversation is with an adult, you have to adapt your speech and manner to those circumstances. You have to listen to the other person and respond in a positive and intelligent manner.

You have to carry the conversation forward, not just sit back and wait for the examiner to do most of the work. Remember, it is you who is expected to do most of the talking.

Try to speak clearly and audibly – do not mumble. When it is necessary, speak in properly constructed sentences and try to avoid bad grammatical errors.

Example

Let's consider an extract from a conversation between an oral examiner and a candidate.

Examiner: So your great passion apart from pop music is netball. Tell me about that.
Janet: It's a good game.
(Silence)
Examiner: What's good about it?
Janet: I just enjoy it.
(Silence)
Examiner: Tell me why.
Janet: I can't really explain. It's just good.
Examiner: Tell me about your hopes for the future.
Janet: What do you mean?
Examiner: Career. Ambitions. That kind of thing.
Janet: I don't know really. I haven't really thought about it.

In this conversation Janet is given the opportunity to talk about two subjects: a game she says she's keen on, and her future hopes. The ball is in her court, but she doesn't take advantage of it. She does not *carry the conversation forward* at all, despite prompting from the examiner. She seems unwilling to expand on her short statements such as 'It's a good game' and 'I just enjoy it'. Her responses make a poor impression, as though she's not really interested in carrying on the conversation. She is not making a real effort to communicate.

Second example
Imagine Janet is given a second chance. The conversation turns out like this:

Examiner: So your great passion apart from pop music is netball. Tell me about that.

Janet: I like taking part in team games like netball. Netball is fast. You have to cover the whole court and there's a lot of skill to the game. Quick passing, dribbling with the ball, shooting for the net. I like winning games, but losing isn't too bad if you think the team has played its best and there's a good feeling about it afterwards.

Examiner: That's interesting. Tell me about your hopes for the future.

Janet: I hope to go to college to do a computer programming course. In fact, that's what I intend to do. We've been doing computer work in school and I've really taken to that and I'm very efficient in handling it. I'd like to get well qualified and find a job with a firm.

Notice how this time Janet responds to the promptings of the examiner. She develops her responses on netball and her future, not needing questions to push her into responding. She carries on the conversation.

Exercise
Practise conversations with adults after having given a prepared talk or reading. Discuss the kinds of subjects mentioned above that an examiner might touch on. Record the conversation and listen to your own contribution carefully and judge if you have:

responded to what has been said to you,
developed your responses enough,
said too much,
carried the conversation forward,
used appropriate speech for the occasion,
spoken clearly and audibly.

ANSWERS TO EXERCISES

Chapter 1
p. 2
1 'It's time to get up,' their mother shouted from downstairs.
2 'There's no need to shout. We're not late,' said Jack.
3 'The cat is wagging its tail,' said Bill. 'That shows it's annoyed.'
4 'I don't know – you're mad. Where are my shoes? They were under my bed. It's a real mystery to me where they get to every morning. I spend a whole hour looking for them. Look at the time – it's half past eight. It's well past the time when I should have left for school.'

p. 4
1 I know whose tie that is. **2** He's too tired to talk to more than two people at a time. **3** I can hear you very well, although the line isn't too good. Who is it who's talking? **4** You can accept or not accept, that's entirely up to you, except there is a certain amount of urgency about this matter, as you know. **5** The effect of your doing that would be to affect what I'm doing. **6** He seemed bored all evening and nearly fell asleep over the games board. **7** To bow to someone is not a sign of weakness. **8** The last episode of the serial was recorded by them on their video and they watched it next morning at breakfast while eating their cereal. **9** What he did must be on his conscience. **10** I am very conscious that I have made a mistake. **11** The current situation is that there is no news at the moment. **12** Put some more currants in this cake.
Passage: He was not conscious when they brought him to the hospital. That much I knew. I was standing there when I happened to hear two doctors talking about his current state of health.

'Who's going to operate?' I could hear one doctor say.

'There's no one on duty except for Johnstone; I must say, if I were him, I wouldn't be too confident.'

After hearing that, I stood with bowed head. The fact that he was lying in hospital close to death lay heavily on my conscience. Whose fault was it? I couldn't accept that I was entirely free from blame. If only he hadn't bored me so much, but that was how he managed to affect me. The question now was what effect the operation would have on him. I knew it would affect me.

p. 5
A recipe for peace is hard to find. No country wants to lose territory whether its claim is just or not. Only through patient negotiation and practice can we hope to achieve any breakthrough. Whether or not we can do so, we cannot be but very thorough in our efforts to put into practice what we preach. We preach peace but prepare to make the world a desert through nuclear war. We must not lay down impossible conditions on our

so-called enemies and expect them to lie down while we trample all over their rights. Until each nation is in receipt of binding rules for peaceful co-existence, then there is no hope for the world and we will get our just deserts.

p. 8

1 When winter comes, birds fall on hard times. Some kind people leave food out for these hardy types that remain behind. However, many small birds die during the harsh, wintry months. If more people were thoughtful enough, more of these lovely small creatures would survive. **2** At that time there was a great deal of industrial trouble. Some people were calling for a general strike. Others wanted settlement by negotiation. The result was chaos. Millions of people were involved. Those not on strike were affected anyway. The atmosphere in the country was very unsettled. **3** Of all the films released that Christmas, there was no doubt which was the most popular. Science fiction films were big box office at that time and this particular example of the genre really drew the crowds. Some of the critics did not review the film very favourably. The public, however, voted with their money. The makers of the film became millionaires almost overnight. **4** Jane couldn't keep up with all the latest dance crazes. One would appear from America, then another one. No sooner had she learnt to do one dance than she felt she had to learn a new dance. Jane prided herself on being up-to-date. She hated the idea of not knowing what the latest thing was. **5** The rain poured down. The umpires had no hesitation in stopping play. The crowd, however, thought differently. They booed the decision. After all, they had paid good money for their match tickets. A little rain was no obstacle to play in their eyes.

p. 9

1 The play consisted of three sections; these were a prologue, a main act and an epilogue. **2** The production also required a large cast: two leading actors, twelve supporting roles and three children. **3** The minister explained his decision: there was no money available; the government was against it anyway; there seemed to be no demand for it. **4** The politician was quoted as saying: 'I have no intention of resigning.' **5** The teacher told the pupils what they had to supply: walking boots, anoraks, sleeping bags and basic utensils. There were to be no exceptions; everybody had to supply his own.

p. 10

1 'Why?' Joan demanded. 'Why does it always have to be me?'
'Because it's the woman's role,' Jack replied.
'Is it now?' Joan exploded. 'In which book of rules did you read that?'
'It's the way of things.' Jack replied.

'Well, I'm neither your mother nor your sister,' Joan stated, 'so cook your own dinner.'

2 'What is your secret as a striker?' the commentator asked. 'Is it your eye for a half chance?'

'I've always been quick,' Bert said. 'I think on my feet, if you know what I mean. Sharp as mustard.'

'You are that,' the commentator agreed, 'Do you ever feel let down after a game?'

'Sick as a parrot, David, sick as a parrot. But then,' he continued, 'I feel over the moon at other times.'

3 'I feel depressed,' Bill said. 'Depressed, depressed, depressed!'

'We all get depressed,' Alec said. 'What's so different about you?'

'I have more reason to be depressed,' Bill continued, 'because I'm broke, I haven't a job and I have to share this flat with you.'

'Charming!' Alec protested. 'Well, you know what you can do.'

'I might just do that,' said Bill.

pp. 12–13

1 Juvenile delinquency is on the increase, we are reliably informed. What, then, is the single main cause for this increase? Perhaps parents no longer control their children. Perhaps children themselves have changed. Or has the period we are living through changed so rapidly that young people are confused by the pace of it all? Whatever the reasons, it seems that the authorities are genuinely concerned. Juvenile delinquency, however, is not a new phenomenon. There have always been complaints about the sins of the younger generation, who in turn become the next generation to complain about the young. It appears it will always be the same.

2 Moving day was an ordeal for all the family. First of all, the van was late. The glass on some picture frames was broken and the cats were reluctant to leave their home. The van men were not particularly co-operative. It appeared they were not really interested in helping. Their time cost enough, that was for sure. Eventually, it was all sorted out and the family was able to move house.

3 Cats are funny animals. They have tremendous pride and show an independence few human beings have. Some people look down on cats, because their brains are said to be small. However, the fact is that cats possess a natural intelligence, a cunning, an alertness; that alone makes them in some ways even more intelligent than humans.

pp. 14–15

1 Because they knew their feeding time to the very minute and seemed to have an in-built instinct about it, the animals were restless. 2 As there was no obvious reason for his anger, the pupils were surprised by it and felt guilty, although they had done nothing. 3 The passengers waited patiently for the bus, as it was very late. Because the snow and ice had made the routes

treacherous, cars were sliding all over the place and driving was an extremely hazardous business. **4** As it had lots of dramatic climaxes and colourful characters, the soap opera was extremely popular with the public. Since it brought some weekly excitement into very drab lives, the programme reached the top of the viewing figures. People of all ages watched it because it was written to have a wide appeal. **5** Because fashion is a business, fashions have to change frequently and it is obvious that designers and clothes manufacturers profit from this.

p. 16
1 There was no reason that I could think of. **2** Quickly she lit the fire, which soon heated up the room. **3** He spoke about France, which he knew nothing about. This infuriated her, because she knew much more. **4** United, who were fourth in the league, had to win the final game which was against the City. They had been playing very badly, which had surprised no one. **5** The woman, who disappeared quickly from the store in Oxford Street, which was very busy at that time, was wearing a red coat. **6** The lawyer, who was very efficient, arranged the purchase of the house, which was in Broomhill Road and in a very quiet district.

p. 18
1 The other boy and I were both very tired. The manager got between my opponent and me; the referee and judge were quick to come to a decision. **2** Between you and them, there is very little to choose. Your education and your natural intelligence give you an advantage, but they have a street-wise attitude to life. As they have had no privileges, the street has taught them to survive. You and I, in comparison, have led very sheltered lives. **3** The old lady admired the bird for its rich plumage and beautiful crested head. The shopkeeper and the old lady were at loggerheads over the price.

pp. 18–19
1 New paragraphs at: 'Hunting is . . .'; 'Of course . . .'.
2 New paragraphs at: 'Not another . . .'; 'It was a familiar . . .'; 'You go by . . .'; 'You know I won't . . .'; 'That's what you always say . . .'; 'That night they went . . .'.

p. 20
1 Louella remarked that, after all, tomorrow was another day. I replied that I didn't care for her philosophy and that tomorrow would creep in at its petty pace. However, Louella persisted in saying that we all had to think of tomorrow, but I replied that I lived for the present. **2** Rocky said that he could have been a champion and a contender. His brother insisted that he had had some money. However, Rocky dismissed this by saying that Charlie didn't understand and that he (Rocky) could have been somebody with some class. He said that Charlie should have looked after him. **3** Nicky

rejected the idea that the old man could go forward to the past and said that he was off his rocker. But the old man insisted that he knew what he was talking about and that he possessed the machine that could go fast forward into the past. Nicky said that surely he meant 'rewind' to the past.

Chapter 2
pp. 35–6 Unmarked example of personal writing
Corrections to errors: friends (line 1); threatening (line 2); hasn't (line 6); question mark (?) after 'friend' (line 7); full stop instead of comma after 'ways', and so capital letter for 'They . . .' (line 9); too inquisitive (line 9); full stop after 'distant', and so capital letter for 'They . . .' (line 10); Everyone has faults *or* Everyone has his or her faults (line 13); ones (line 18); full stop instead of comma after 'are', and so capital letter for 'Happy . . .' (line 23; process (line 26); 'has' instead of 'have brought you' (line 37); often (line 38); quite (line 56).

pp. 48–9 Unmarked example of argumentative writing
Corrections to errors: popular (line 1); seems (line 11); no (line 14); stories (line 15); defenders . . . point (line 28); society (line 46).

pp. 64–5 Unmarked example of narrative writing
Corrections to errors: roughly (line 4); embarrassed (line 11); murmured (line 15); full stop instead of comma after 'there', and so capital letter for 'His . . .' (line 20); said (line 59).

pp. 77–8 Unmarked example of descriptive writing
Corrections to errors: vivacity (line 17); semi-colon instead of comma after 'me' (line 23); Elsa's (line 28); reliability, character, practical (line 29); tornadoes (line 37); often (line 42); semi-colon (or full stop) instead of comma after 'room' (line 42); full stop instead of comma after 'birthday' (line 43).

ACKNOWLEDGEMENTS

The author and publishers are grateful to the following for permission to reproduce copyright material in this book:

The *Advertising Standards Authority* for one extract (pp. 96–7) from their advertisement which appeared in the *Sunday Express Magazine* on 24th July 1984; *Caryl Churchill*: one extract (pp. 149–50) from *Top Girls*, reprinted by permission of Methuen, London; *Brendan Gill*: one extract (pp. 141–2) from *Truth and Consequences*, reprinted from *Ways of Loving* © 1941 by Brendan Gill by permission of Harcourt Brace Jovanovich, Inc.; *Maxim Gorki*, for one extract (pp. 135–6) from *My Childhood* in the translation edited by D. Holbrook, reprinted by permission of Cambridge University Press; *Graham Greene*, for one extract (pp. 153–4) from *Brighton Rock*, reprinted by permission of William Heinemann Ltd and The Bodley Head Ltd; *Lillian Hellman*, for one extract (pp. 125–6) from *Pentimento*, reprinted by permission of Quartet Books Ltd, London; *Rosemary Joseph* for *Baking Day* (pp. 146–7), reprinted by permission of the author; *Doris Lessing*, for one extract (pp. 155–6) from *The Four-Gated City*, reprinted by permission of the Collins Publishing Group; *The Midland Bank*, for one extract (p. 99) advertising material on Budget accounts; the *Morning Star*, for one extract (p. 139); *Shiva Naipaul*, for one extract (pp. 117–8) from *Beyond the Dragon's Mouth*, © Shiva Naipaul 1984, reprinted by permission of Hamish Hamilton Ltd; *Rukshana Smith*, for one extract (pp. 126–7) from *Sumitra's Story*, reprinted by permission of Macmillan, London and Basingstoke; the *Sunday Express Magazine*, for one extract (pp. 94–5); the *Sunday Times*, for extracts from the following articles: *How Frankie built their pleasure dome* by Jon Savage (4 November 1984) (p. 157); the Bestsellers column (31 March 1985) (pp. 109–10); *Europe honours the unknown Songster*, by Stephen Pile (5 May 1985) (pp. 156–7); *Bird lovers brave Islay's wrath again* by Sarah Helm and George Rosie (p. 120), and a report on the British summer by Tim Rayment (11 May 1985) (pp. 122–3); *The Stable Lad* by Caroline Silver and *The Bookie* by Nick Pitt (10 June 1986) (pp. 131–2); *Thomson Holidays* for one extract (pp. 91–2) from 1984/85 Winter Sun brochure; *The Times* for extracts from two articles: *Pit police face petrol bombs in 7 hour fury*, by Peter Davenport (p. 138), and *A habit that's going up in smoke*, by Derek Harris (22 April 1985) (pp. 105–6); *Fay Weldon*, for one extract (p. 136) from *The Life and Loves of a She-Devil*, reprinted by permission of the author's agents, Anthony Shield.